ETHICS FOR ROBOTS

Ethics for Robots describes and defends a method for designing and evaluating ethics algorithms for autonomous machines, such as self-driving cars and search and rescue drones. Derek Leben argues that such algorithms should be evaluated by how effectively they accomplish the problem of cooperation among self-interested organisms, and therefore, rather than simulating the psychological systems that have evolved to solve this problem, engineers should be tackling the problem itself, taking relevant lessons from our moral psychology.

Leben draws on the moral theory of John Rawls, arguing that normative moral theories are attempts to develop optimal solutions to the problem of cooperation. He claims that Rawlsian Contractarianism leads to the 'Maximin' principle – the action that maximizes the minimum value – and that the Maximin principle is the most effective solution to the problem of cooperation. He contrasts the Maximin principle with other principles and shows how they can often produce non-cooperative results.

Using real-world examples – such as an autonomous vehicle facing a situation where every action results in harm, home care machines, and autonomous weapons systems – Leben contrasts Rawlsian algorithms with alternatives derived from utilitarianism and natural rights libertarianism.

Including chapter summaries and a glossary of technical terms, *Ethics for Robots* is essential reading for philosophers, engineers, computer scientists, and cognitive scientists working on the problem of ethics for autonomous systems.

Derek Leben is Associate Professor of Philosophy, University of Pittsburgh Johnstown, USA.

ETHICS FOR ROBOTS

How to Design a Moral Algorithm

Derek Leben

LONDON AND NEW YORK

First published 2019
by Routledge
2 Park Square, Milton Park, Abingdon, Oxon OX14 4RN

and by Routledge
711 Third Avenue, New York, NY 10017

Routledge is an imprint of the Taylor & Francis Group, an informa business

© 2019 Derek Leben

The right of Derek Leben to be identified as author of this work has been asserted by him in accordance with sections 77 and 78 of the Copyright, Designs and Patents Act 1988.

All rights reserved. No part of this book may be reprinted or reproduced or utilised in any form or by any electronic, mechanical, or other means, now known or hereafter invented, including photocopying and recording, or in any information storage or retrieval system, without permission in writing from the publishers.

Trademark notice: Product or corporate names may be trademarks or registered trademarks, and are used only for identification and explanation without intent to infringe.

British Library Cataloguing-in-Publication Data
A catalogue record for this book is available from the British Library

Library of Congress Cataloging-in-Publication Data
Names: Leben, Derek, author.
Title: Ethics for robots: how to design a moral algorithm / Derek Leben.
Description: Abingdon, Oxon; New York, NY: Routledge, 2018. |
Includes bibliographical references and index.
Identifiers: LCCN 2018007376 | ISBN 9781138716155 (hbk: alk. paper) |
ISBN 9781138716179 (pbk: alk. paper) | ISBN 9781315197128 (ebk)
Subjects: LCSH: Robotics–Moral and ethical aspects. |
Robotics–Safety measures.
Classification: LCC TJ211.28 .L43 2018 | DDC 174/.9629892–dc23
LC record available at https://lccn.loc.gov/2018007376

ISBN: 978-1-138-71615-5 (hbk)
ISBN: 978-1-138-71617-9 (pbk)
ISBN: 978-1-315-19712-8 (ebk)

Typeset in Bembo
by Deanta Global Publishing Services, Chennai, India

Printed and bound in Great Britain by
TJ International Ltd, Padstow, Cornwall

Dedicated to Sean and Ethan

CONTENTS

Acknowledgments viii

    Introduction 1

1 Moral psychology 7

2 Cooperation problems 25

3 Theories 42

4 Contractarianism 59

5 Ethics engines 76

6 Avoiding collisions 97

7 Saving lives 116

8 Keeping the peace 130

    Conclusions 146

Glossary *151*
Index *155*

ACKNOWLEDGMENTS

Thanks to David Danks, Jeff Maynes, and Michael Cox for helpful feedback.

And thanks to the 61B café for being a good place to write a book.

INTRODUCTION

The word *robot* was coined by the Czech playwright and journalist Karel Capek in his 1920 play, *Rossum's Universal Robots*. The play is about a company that creates biological human workers that don't have a soul, so they can take over all the jobs that humans usually do. If this idea seemed far-fetched in the 1920s, it doesn't seem that way today. Machines are rapidly taking over tasks that were previously performed by humans in every domain of our society, including agriculture, factory production, transportation, medicine, retail sales, finance, education, and even warfare. Most of these machines have simple programs that allow them to automatically perform a single repetitive task like welding car doors, scanning products, or vacuuming the floor. Gradually, machines are beginning to also take over tasks which involve weighing several different options to arrive at a decision, like driving, diagnosing diseases, and responding to threats. Let's call these kinds of tasks *complex*. For our purposes, a robot is any physically embodied machine that can perform complex tasks without any direct human intervention.

According to this definition, a robot doesn't necessarily have to look like a human. For instance, I'll consider driverless cars and certain kinds of missile systems to be robots. The key feature of a robot is that it is *autonomous*, which means making decisions based on principles or reasoning without direct human intervention. Autonomy has a special meaning in moral philosophy; it's not just being able to act in response to input (this might be called *automatic*), but instead, being able to think and make decisions in a responsible way. This requires a minimal kind of artificial intelligence, but I will consider AI to be a broader class of systems that are not necessarily embodied and more general in the scope of their abilities. The robots that we're most interested in are machines that operate dangerous vehicles or equipment, perform medical services, and provide security. These machines will be making decisions that could result in harm to others, which is why we need a framework for designing ethical robots.

One early proposal for a robot ethics originated in the science-fiction stories of Isaac Asimov. Asimov's three laws of robotics are:

1. A robot may not harm a human being or, through inaction, allow a human being to come to harm.
2. A robot must obey orders given it by human beings except where such orders would conflict with the First Law.
3. A robot must protect its own existence, as long as such protection does not conflict with the First or Second Law.

These principles seem appealing at first, and they work well enough as a rough guideline for most normal situations. It's no coincidence that the first rule looks like the "golden rule" that's been repeated throughout cultural and religious traditions from Confucianism to Christianity.

Even though "don't cause or allow harm" is good as a rough guideline for behavior, it won't work as a detailed rule for decision-making. One major problem is that this law is useless until we define what counts as *harm*. Is it harming someone to insult them, lie to them, or trespass on their property? What about actions that violate a person's consent or dignity? Some actions are only likely to cause harm, but what's the threshold for *likely* harm? Every action could *possibly* lead to harm, so failing to specify this threshold will leave robots paralyzed with fear, unable to perform even the most basic of tasks.

Another problem with a rule like "don't cause or allow harm" is that it immediately breaks down once we venture to situations where *every* action leads to harm for a human being, even the action of doing nothing at all. These cases are called moral dilemmas. Although moral dilemmas aren't common, they *do happen*, and they can be disturbingly frequent in fields like medicine and warfare. Doctors must sometimes decide between respecting a patient's wishes and doing what's best for her health. Soldiers must sometimes decide between killing defenseless enemies and allowing civilians to die. Moral dilemmas are cases where harms to one person or group are inevitable, so an agent must decide which harm is worse. What we need is a more specific way to define and weigh harms.

Asimov's laws might be called a "top-down" approach to programming ethical robots, where we use a set of rigid rules to constrain and guide behavior. An alternative approach, which is sometimes called "bottom-up," uses machine learning techniques to change a robot's behavior in response to positive or negative feedback. It's true that some of the most impressive examples of machines performing complex human tasks in the past decade have used this kind of reinforcement learning within a multilayered network of flexible artificial neurons. For instance, in 2010, the Stanford computer scientist Fei-Fei Li began an annual competition where competitors would each submit their object recognition algorithms to be tested against the most massive database of images in the world, called ImageNet. The algorithms were compared based on performance on tasks like recognition and classification. The human error rate on these tasks is about

5–6 percent. In 2010, the winning algorithm had an error rate of 28 percent. In 2011, the error rate was 25 percent. Then, in 2012, the introduction of "deep learning" techniques produced a winning algorithm with an error rate of just 15 percent. Since then, the winner has improved its accuracy every year, with the 2015 algorithm having an error rate of 3.5 percent, which is better than human judgment. If machine learning can simulate human performance at recognizing images, using language, and driving vehicles, why not moral judgments?

The challenge for a machine learning approach to designing robot ethics is that choices must be made about what kind of information is used as positive or negative feedback. If we are using human judgments to model machine judgments, then robots will inevitably incorporate the biases and inconsistencies in our own psychology: preference for people who are familiar or genetically related, ignoring the effects of our actions on people who are very distant, and relying on false beliefs about what kinds of actions are harmful. A considerable number of human beings over the course of history have been raised to approve of horrible things like genocide, rape, slavery, torture, and child abuse, to name just a few. Even if we take historical exemplars like Aristotle as our training set, a well-respected model citizen in Aristotle's homeland of fourth-century (BC) Macedonia would probably be a slave-holding pedophile. My point is that we can't simply point a machine learning network at human behavior and shout: "Learn!" Instead, machine learning approaches will need to make important theoretical assumptions about what kinds of data are morally important.

The aim of this book is to provide a general theoretical framework for designing moral algorithms, whether they be "top-down" or "bottom-up." Many of the engineers and scientists working on this problem don't have training in ethics, and don't seem to think that they need any. However, it's impossible to design an ethics procedure for machines without making substantial theoretical assumptions about how we solve moral problems. Perhaps the only way to objectively solve moral problems is by understanding the *function* of morality. Armed with a proper understanding of the practical function of morality, we can turn to the engineering task of designing an artificial system that performs this same function just as well as humans, if not better.

How can a machine be *better* at making moral decisions than a human being? In the twenty-first century, most of us have no problem acknowledging that computers can make better decisions than an average human when it comes to games or calculations, but how could a machine ever surpass us in something so fundamentally human as *moral decisions*? This response reveals an important assumption: that morality is essentially a product of our own minds, and somehow limited to human beings. In philosophy, the term for this position is "anti-realism," as opposed to "realism." The choice between realism or anti-realism turns out to be the most important initial assumption in any discussion about ethics.

If moral realism is false, and there are no objective mind-independent answers to moral questions, then ethics is about a set of psychological responses and cultural traditions. None of these responses and traditions would be inherently better or worse than the other. There would be no "correct" answers to moral questions. In designing robot ethics, programmers could be accused of incorporating their own biases involving gender, sexual orientation, race, religion, or cultural tradition. Ethics would become a kind of identity politics, where each group lobbies against the other to try to have their own intuitions and favorite principles represented. This approach is just as disastrous in ethics as it is in politics. In Plato's *Republic*, he describes the "democratic man," who is pushed and pulled about by competing internal interests, never having a general rule that manages and guides these interests. This person is in desperate need of a unifying framework for tying these interests together, which we call a *constitution*. If programmers design robots to be a sampler platter of various moral intuitions and principles, they risk creating a real-life version of Plato's democratic man, lacking any constitution to its decisions.

On the other hand, if morality has adapted in response to a practical problem, then there might exist an objective and mind-independent set of solutions to this problem. In this kind of moral realism, we can survey human psychology and culture in a context of discovery, as we explore the possible landscape of attempted solutions. Ultimately, though, some solutions are objectively better than others. In principle, solutions to the problem of cooperation could be generated without reference to any historical traditions, texts, or intuitions.

My training is in "Western" philosophy, so in this book, I'll be mostly discussing figures like Plato, Hume, Kant, and Rawls. I'll suggest that one moral theory, Contractarianism, provides the best solution to the problem of cooperation. I wouldn't be surprised if this solution has been independently discovered in different cultures, as is often the case in the history of science and mathematics. The reason that I won't be discussing these non-Western traditions is not cultural bias or insensitivity; instead, it's a commitment to moral realism, and the idea that solutions to moral problems are engineering problems, like constructing a bridge. We can certainly gain inspiration from bridge-building traditions in ancient China, India, and the Americas, but this isn't essential to solving the problem. Ultimately, the solutions to moral problems are transcendent of culture. This also entails the conclusion that robots might not only surpass us in their abilities to solve moral problems, but also help us understand our own limitations.

It's not just philosophers who can help engineers; the relationship is a two-way street. Designing algorithms for machine behavior can help us gain focus in guiding human behavior. Philosophers sometimes forget about the need for concrete rules in decision-making. There's a famous story about a student who approached the philosopher Jean-Paul Sartre asking for advice. The student's brother had gone off to fight in the French Resistance, leaving him to stay behind and care for their ailing mother. Despite this obligation to take care of his mother, the student also felt a strong obligation to go off and fight for his brother and country. Sartre's response was: "You are free, therefore choose – that is to say invent. No rule of general morality can show you what you ought to do: no signs are vouchsafed in this world." I imagine that the student's response was a sarcastic: "Great, thanks." There are many moral theories that make vague claims about one being a *virtuous person* and expressing *care* for other people, but these theories don't provide any practical guidelines for actions. Thinking about how we would program a machine to be "virtuous" or "caring" illustrates how useless these moral theories can be. It forces us to be specific in ways that we've never been forced to be, and to do the hard work needed to produce a real decision-procedure, not just for machines but for ourselves.

The first half of this book will survey approaches to modeling ethics algorithms based on (1) universal features of human moral psychology, (2) successful strategies in cooperation games, and (3) historically influential moral theories. All of these approaches are promising, but what is needed is an overarching theoretical framework tying them together. If we view them as linked together by *functionality*, it will enable us to take the parts of each approach that work and ignore the parts that are irrelevant. Specifically, I'll argue that our moral intuitions are the product of a psychological network that adapted in response to the problem of enforcing cooperative behavior among self-interested organisms. Moral theories are (sometimes unconscious) attempts to clarify and generalize these intuitive judgments. Once we view both moral intuitions and theories as goal-directed, it's possible to objectively evaluate which features are most effective at accomplishing this goal. As the most effective solution to cooperation problems, Contractarianism contains the universal features of our moral psychology and extends them consistently to non-cooperative contexts like moral dilemmas. It provides a detailed way of determining which objects are valuable, what kinds of actions are harmful, and the importance of concepts like rights and consent, as well as providing a general rule called the Maximin principle that can produce a unique decision in even the most difficult of moral dilemmas. If you aren't convinced by my arguments that ethics is connected to cooperation problems, the rest of the book is still valuable: you can just think of it as "cooperation for robots" instead.

The second half of the book will examine how Contractarianism can be turned into a program for autonomous machines. Using chess engines as a model, I describe how an ethics engine based on Contractarianism would operate, what its algorithms might look like, and how this procedure applies to decisions made by robots in various domains. The domains include transportation, saving lives, and keeping the peace. There are many important questions about robot ethics that aren't discussed here. These questions include: "Under what conditions is a robot morally responsible for its actions?" "Who do we hold responsible when a robot misbehaves?" "When, if ever, does a robot become a person with rights?" "What are the social, economic, and legal implications of allowing robots to take over more of our decision-making?" Instead, the focus of this book is: "*If* we are going to build autonomous robots in domains like transportation, medicine, and war, here are the moral principles that should constrain their decisions." This leaves open whether autonomous robots can ever be genuinely responsible, worthy of rights, or even a good idea to build in the first place. My suspicion is that full automation is a good idea in domains like transportation, but a bad idea in domains like warfare. I am also generally optimistic that increasing the presence of autonomous machines into our society and economy will produce beneficial results, providing greater wealth, leisure, and security for even the worst-off members of the population. However, I have been wrong before.

Designing ethical machines is an interdisciplinary project, and this book will draw on work in math, biology, economics, philosophy, computer science, and cognitive science. I will start by apologizing to each of these fields, because I'm going to oversimplify topics that require volumes to address in detail. This even includes my own field of philosophy; I'll often be squeezing important debates that span centuries of time and volumes of texts into a single page or even a single paragraph. I'm painfully aware of the extent to which these topics are being condensed and often oversimplified. However, given that I am trying to present a broad theoretical framework here in an accessible and compact format, I hope that the philosophers will forgive me as well.

The goal of interdisciplinary research is to tie together work in different fields in a new way, leading to unexpected results. I've tried to write the book at a level that makes it accessible to any motivated reader. Mathematical details and intimidating symbols have been left out or pushed to endnotes. Any graphs or formal expressions that I've left in the main text should be accessible to anyone with even the most basic math background, and I encourage you to spend a minute or two working through them. Many people don't have the time or the attention span to read an entire book. Don't feel bad about it. I've tried to make each chapter somewhat independent, so feel free to skip around. For better or worse, every citizen of the industrialized world must now take an interest in robot decision-making, and the people working on them should be trying to bring the conversation to the public as much as possible.

1

MORAL PSYCHOLOGY

Harry Truman had only been the vice-president for 82 days when, on April 12, 1945, Franklin Roosevelt died. Truman became the 33rd president at the end of World War II, when the Japanese Empire had been pushed back to its mainland islands, and preparations were being made for the Allied invasion of Japan. The planned invasion, called Operation Downfall, was estimated to last for years and cost perhaps half a million American lives, along with millions more Japanese casualties.

Just 13 days after taking office, the U.S. Secretary of War, Henry Stimson, sent Truman a letter describing a "secret matter" that "I think you ought to know about ... without delay." This secret was the atomic bomb, which had been the product of secret research conducted at the Los Alamos research site. Within just a few months of learning about what he called "the most terrible bomb in the history of the world," Truman now faced a monumental decision: would he allow the planned invasion of Japan to continue its deadly course, costing millions of lives, or deliberately drop atomic bombs on Japanese cities, at a cost of maybe only a few hundred thousand lives, to force the enemy into unconditional surrender?

Truman chose to drop the atomic bomb, first on Hiroshima (August 6) and then on Nagasaki (August 9). The death tolls are estimated at 90,000–120,000 for Hiroshima, and 60,000–80,000 for Nagasaki, the majority of both being civilian deaths. Thousands of innocent men, women, and children were immediately killed by the blast, and thousands more died over the following weeks from radiation exposure. On August 12, Japan declared unconditional surrender. There has been intense debate since the bombing as to whether the decision was morally acceptable. Public opinion has shifted dramatically over time, with Pew polls suggesting that 85 percent of Americans approving of the bombing in 1945, but only 57 percent of Americans approving in 2016. Critics argue that Japan was already looking for a way to end the war, and that there were other options that could have forced them to surrender without dropping additional bombs. For the sake of this discussion, let's assume that these really were the *only* two options: either invade Japan at a cost of millions of lives, or drop bombs on two mostly civilian populations at a cost of hundreds of thousands of lives. Which is the right decision?

To those of you familiar with moral philosophy, you'll recognize a similarity here to one of the most famous thought-experiments in ethics, called the *trolley problem*, originally developed by philosophers Philippa Foot (1967) and Judith Thomson (1976). In the standard version of the trolley problem, a runaway train is heading towards five people, but you can save them by diverting the train to a side-track. Unfortunately, there is a single person on the side-track who will certainly die as a result of pulling the switch (Figure 1.1).

There's a reason why the trolley problem has been a useful tool for philosophers and psychologists; dilemmas like these can reveal the inner workings of the way that we make moral judgments. According to Mikhail's (2011) extensive cross-cultural surveys, most people surveyed on this question think the right decision is to pull the switch. You might think that the reason for pulling the switch is obvious: pick the action that saves the most lives. However, when presented with an alternate scenario, where it's necessary to push a large man in front of the train to save five people (Figure 1.2), almost everybody rejects it as morally wrong. This is strange, since the "save the most lives" principle predicts that pushing a man in front of a train is no different from diverting the train to kill a pedestrian; both actions are sacrificing one to save five. It's obvious from this example that actual moral judgments are more complicated than we thought.

Trolley Problem (Bystander)

States	P1	P2	P3	P4	P5	P6
Do Nothing	0	−99	−99	−99	−99	−99
Pull Switch	−99	0	0	0	0	0

FIGURE 1.1 Payoffs in the Trolley Problem (bystander version), measured in terms of changes from each player's current state. For instance, 0 means you experience no change from your current state, while −100 is a maximal loss from your current state. For now, these numbers don't matter, we can call them a percentage of loss. Let's say that getting hit by a train will lead to a 99 percent chance of losing everything that's important. P1 is the person on the side-track, and P2–P6 are the five people on the main track.

Moral psychology

Trolley Problem (Footbridge)

States	P1	P2	P3	P4	P5	P6
Do Nothing	0	−99	−99	−99	−99	−99
Pull Man	−99	0	0	0	0	0

FIGURE 1.2 Payoffs in the Trolley Problem (footbridge version). P1 is the man on the bridge, and P2–P6 are the five people on the main track.

This chapter will give a broad survey of the universal categories and rules that people use when making moral judgments. We'll see that moral judgments are a unique system in the human mind, distinct from social conventions, emotions, and religious beliefs. I'll be calling this a *functional network* to emphasize that our system for making moral judgments is probably a collection of older psychological capacities that have been co-opted over time for a single practical purpose. Many researchers who are developing ethics algorithms for machines view moral judgment as a cognitive trait like language, and the obvious way to implement this trait in a machine is to simulate our moral grammar. I'll try to show how our moral psychology carries along with it many useful features, but also many unfortunate ones that we don't want to program into robots. The following chapters will develop a framework for determining exactly which of these features are useful or unfortunate.

Moral grammar

Any survey of human universals, like that compiled by anthropologist Donald Brown (1991), will include the fact that all human beings judge some actions as wrong and others as permissible. It's not hard to think of actions that most of us intuitively categorize as morally wrong: homicide, battery, rape, abuse, discrimination, cheating, and massive deception. These judgments are made quickly, automatically, and without effort. If I were to ask you *why* you think that cheating is wrong, you might be baffled and find it hard to answer. You might even say: "It just is!" This doesn't mean that there are no rules for evaluating right and wrong, but it suggests that these rules are unconscious, like asking someone why they perceive a table as rectangular or why they accept a sentence as grammatical. The job of moral psychology is to discover how people understand the categories of *wrong* and *acceptable*, and how they sort actions into these categories.

Skeptics about morality may question whether there is a unique kind of thing called a *moral judgment*. Here are some ways of thinking that morality is really something else entirely:

- "Morality is nothing more than a set of social conventions like etiquette and laws!"
- "Morality is nothing more than a set of religious commands!"
- "Morality is nothing more than an expression of people's emotions!"

It's true that social conventions, religion, and emotions are strongly associated with moral judgments. But, as social scientists say, correlation isn't causation. In order to talk about morality, we'll start by distinguishing it from these closely related phenomena.

Social conventions like "men have short hair and women wear dresses" are used to guide people's behavior, but the rules themselves are arbitrary and vary widely from culture to culture. A famous (and probably apocryphal) story of the Persian Emperor Darius describes how the ancient Indians in his court judged eating their dead parents to be a sign of great respect, while the ancient Greeks found it to be a sign of great offense. The typical conclusion from stories like this is that morality is an arbitrary set of rules, and there's no common ground we can use to settle disagreements, so we should just be tolerant of all moral beliefs.

In response to this story, the philosopher James Rachels (2009) points out that there is a lot more agreement about moral beliefs than social conventions. In the story of Darius, both the Indians and Greeks agreed on the more general rule: honor your parents. They just disagreed about which practice is the best way of honoring them, eating or not eating them. It's important to keep in mind how a person's empirical beliefs about how the world works can dramatically change her moral judgments. For example, torturing an innocent person may look like a barbaric practice to us, but if the people doing it genuinely believe that this action is saving the person's immortal soul from an eternity of torture, or saving an entire society from the wrath of the gods, then the judgment begins to look less crazy. Ask yourself how your moral beliefs would change if you were to genuinely *believe* that a cow could contain the soul of your dead parents, or that some group intentionally caused the diseases your family is experiencing. Barbaric actions often turn out to be based on the same moral principles that we endorse, but tragically incorrect information about how the world works.

Even if a distant society approves of slavery and child abuse, hopefully you still think these actions are morally wrong. Tolerance is a good attitude to have about social conventions, but it's a disastrous policy to have about moral beliefs. Several decades ago, the developmental psychologist Elliot Turiel (1983) and his colleagues conducted experiments where some groups of children were told stories about conventional rule violations ("Is it okay to wear pajamas to school if teacher says so?") and other groups of children were told stories about moral rule violations ("Is it okay to hit another student if teacher says so?"). Five-year-old children tend to accept that social norm violations are acceptable when a teacher approves of it, but actions like hitting another child are typically judged to be wrong, even if an authority or other community approves.

This distinction between ethics and authority is something advocated by philosophers from Plato to Kant. It's true that there are laws against attacking strangers, but it would be ridiculous to say that the *reason* you don't punch strangers in the face is that you're worried about getting arrested! Similarly, there are religious commands against murder, lying, and stealing, but it's strange to say that Christians or Muslims would suddenly become more violent if not for religious laws. The rate of violent behavior among atheists is no different than the rate of violence among religious followers, and there is no difference between atheists and religious people in their responses to scenarios like the trolley problem. In 2011, U.S. Senator Trent Franks accidentally made this point clear when he defended the motto of the United States, "In God We Trust," by arguing that without a trust in God, the country would collapse into violent chaos:

> An atheist state is as brutal as the thesis that it rests upon, and there is no reason for us to gather in this place [the U.S. Chamber of Commerce], we should just let anarchy prevail, because after all, we are just worm food.

This speech was mocked by *The Daily Show* host Jon Stewart, who continued to fill in the logical consequences of the senator's comment:

> I guess what I'm saying here, Mister Speaker, is that this four-word motto is right now the only thing standing between me and a nihilistic killing spree of epic proportions. Seriously, I just want to state for the congressional record: I do not know right from wrong.

The audience laughed at this joke because they recognized that basing your moral beliefs entirely on what someone else tells you is a childish attitude which leads to absurd conclusions. In a dramatic example, Immanuel Kant (1798) wrote of the story of Abraham and Isaac:

> [In] the myth of the sacrifice that Abraham was going to make by butchering and burning his only son at God's command ... Abraham should have replied to this supposedly divine voice: "That I ought not kill my good son is quite certain. But that you, this apparition, are God – of that I am not certain, and never can be, not even if this voice rings down to me from the (visible) heaven."

Kant was an *extremely* devoted religious believer, and he's saying to basically ignore the commands of God when it comes to ethics. Millions of religious believers also regularly ignore the teachings of authority figures over issues they believe are right or wrong. Despite the Catholic Church insisting that contraception is morally wrong, a 2014 Pew poll found that 79 percent of Catholics believe it to be permissible. Drastic changes in moral beliefs seem to have no obvious connection to religious beliefs; between 2007 and 2014, Pew research shows that all religious and non-religious groups in the United States changed their views about the permissibility of homosexuality at roughly the same rate. Even Mormons and Evangelical Christians show a change from 24–26 percent to 36 percent acceptance of homosexuality, despite no clear difference in the commands of their churches. Religion certainly has an influence on what sorts of information people are exposed to, but there's no reason to think this has any *greater* influence on moral beliefs than other sources of information. There are similar religious differences in beliefs about evolution and global warming, but it's silly to think that religion is the *cause* of beliefs about global warming, or that beliefs about global warming are nothing more than religious attitudes.

What about emotions? If I judge an action to be morally wrong, I will almost certainly feel upset about it, angry at people who do it, and motivated to avoid doing that action. You would think it's crazy if someone believes an action is morally wrong and feels *happy* about people doing it. Philosophers like David Hume (1738) have used this connection to argue that emotions are the ultimate cause of moral judgments. His argument is that morality always involves motivation, and the only source of motivation is the emotions, so morality must originate (at least in part) from human emotions. As Hume summarizes:

> [I]t is impossible that the distinction betwixt moral good and evil can be made by reason; since that distinction has an influence on our actions, of which reason alone is incapable.

I agree with Hume that the emotions play an important role in moral judgments, but there's a big difference between playing a role in morality and being *all there is* to morality. An example of this radical view is found in A.J. Ayer's theory (1936) that words like *wrong* are nothing more than expressions of emotions:

> [I]f I say to someone, "you acted wrongly in stealing that money," … It is as if I had said, "you stole that money," in a peculiar tone of horror, or written if with the addition of some special exclamation marks. The tone, or the exclamation marks, adds nothing to the literal meaning of the sentence. It merely serves to show that the expression is attended by certain feelings of that speaker.

Ayer's speculation about the meaning of words like *ought* and *wrong* has turned out to be incorrect. Our best linguistic theories about the meaning of words like *ought* show that they are operators acting like the words *all* and *some*. There are patterns in the way that people use moral terms that are identical to patterns in the way people use *all* and *some*. For example, everyone accepts the inferences:

1. Every baby gets sick =
It's false that some babies don't get sick
2. Not every baby is cute =
Some babies aren't cute
3. Every baby is loveable ⇒
Therefore, (at least) some babies are loveable.

It turns out that if we make the connection: [all = obligatory] and [some = permissible], then the same patterns show up in inferences with moral terms:

1. Jonathon must be in his office =
It's not acceptable for Jonathon not to be in his office
2. Jonathon doesn't have to be in his office =
It's acceptable for Jonathon to not be in his office
3. Jonathon must be in his office ⇒
Therefore, it's (at least) acceptable that Jonathon is in his office.[1]

Why would it be that patterns in moral terms act like *all* and *some*? The typical answer that linguists like Angelika Kratzer (1977) suggest is that these words involve the same basic operations, called universal and existential quantification. Call these operators P for "permissible" and O for "obligated," so that O[Jonathon is in his office] means "Jonathon is obligated to be in his office." There is an entire field called *deontic logic* devoted entirely to the study of these operators. We won't get into the details here, but the point is that any information under the scope of these kinds of operators has to have a very specific kind of structure that involves predicates and connectives. This shows that moral judgments must be more than merely emotional responses, although emotions may play a very important role in determining how certain actions are classified as permissible or required (this is similar to an argument initially developed by the philosophers Gottlob Frege and Peter Geach).

Instead of thinking about moral judgments as social conventions, religious beliefs, or emotional responses, a better analogy is to think of them as a functional network like human language. In his book, *Elements of Moral Cognition* (2011), John Mikhail describes this analogy in detail. Just like our quick and automatic responses about grammar, judgments about the permissibility of actions are the product of a set of rules about which speakers are largely unconscious. Mikhail calls this set of rules *moral grammar*. The study of moral grammar investigates the categories and rules used by speakers to move from perceptions of actions to judgments about permissibility or impermissibility.

One way that the linguistic analogy is helpful is that it shows how we can appeal to our own intuitions as evidence about the unconscious psychological processes that produced them. This is one of the many changes that Noam Chomsky brought to linguistics during the 1950s and 1960s. The analogy also shows how speakers can be making use of unconscious rules that *they themselves* can't explicitly describe. For example, as competent English speakers, we can easily transform the sentence *John is running* into *Is John running?* but most of us are incapable of explaining the rule for this: "Move the first aux verb after the subject to the front; if there is no aux verb, insert a do/does." This is fascinating: it's a rule that we all use but can't explicitly articulate. Moral rules seem to have a similar ineffable quality to them; they're easy to use but hard to explain. As U.S. Supreme Court Justice Potter Stewart famously remarked about obscenity:

> I shall not today attempt further to define the kinds of material I understand to be expressed within that shorthand description [hardcore pornography], and perhaps I could never succeed in intelligibly doing so. But I know it when I see it…

As much as this remark has been mocked over the years, it's the same quality that linguistic rules have: I can't articulate what makes a sentence of my native language grammatical or ungrammatical, but I know a well-constructed one when I see it. This isn't because the rules are part of some magical realm that we can only detect with extrasensory perception. Instead, it's because these rules are structures in our minds and brains; we have conscious access only to their outputs. With enough careful study, we can hypothesize about and reconstruct what rules our brains are using to form grammatical sentences and sort actions into categories of wrong and acceptable.

In human languages, it is truly incredible how a massive amount of variation can be generated from toggling parameters on a few simple underlying rules. This insight can be framed as a way of answering the "nature/nurture" question for a cognitive trait. As Steven Pinker (2002) points out, the boring (and almost trivially true) answer to this question is "a little bit of both," but the interesting answer is describing in detail exactly *how* innate features of the human mind enable parts of language to be acquired through experience. According to the linguistic analogy, some components of our moral judgments, like what objects are valuable and which effects are harmful, may be acquired through emotional responses and cultural norms. However, the way that valuable objects and harmful effects are framed within a system of rules may be constrained by only a limited set of configurations determined by the structure of our moral psychology.

As the cognitive scientist David Marr (1981) argued, there are at least three distinct levels of explanation for a cognitive trait like language or moral judgment: (1) the way a system is implemented, (2) the categories and rules it uses, and (3) the goal of the system. For example, a cash register is implemented in the hardware of the machine, it uses a few basic computational rules, and the function of the machine is to report prices and exchange money. If morality is a functional network of the human mind, we want to know how it's implemented in the brain, the rules that it's using to evaluate actions, and what its historical function is. I'll have nothing to say about how moral judgments are implemented in the human brain, but the rest of this chapter will discuss some of the abstract entities and rules that the moral network uses, and the next chapter will look at its evolutionary and historical function.

Elements of moral grammar

Psychologists Fiery Cushman and Joshua Greene (2012) have argued that moral dilemmas are useful because they smash our normal moral intuitions together, allowing us to see what pieces they're made of, like high-energy particle collisions. Researchers like Mikhail predict that manipulating dilemmas will reveal a small set of elements, like the following[2]:

AGENT
PATIENT
INTEND
CAUSE
STATE
HARM

Like any good theory, we want to get the smallest number of elements necessary to build up all the bigger structures from them. A good theory of chemistry will have elements like *hydrogen* and *oxygen*, then build larger structures like water molecules. Similarly, the hope of a computational theory of moral grammar is that all moral beliefs and even more complex concepts like *innocence* and *consent* can be built as molecules from these basic elements.

Let's start with AGENT and PATIENT. Just like it's hard to build a sentence without a noun and a direct object, it's equally hard to make a moral judgment without an agent and a patient. Roughly, agents are the ones who perform the action and patients are the ones who experience its effects. In their book, *The Mind Club* (2016), psychologists Daniel Wegner and Kurt Gray describe some of the features that humans use to detect what objects are agents and patients. While people reliably identify normal adult humans as both agents *and* patients, some objects are only identified as agents (gods and robots), while others are only identified as patients (cute animals and babies). Wegner and Gray hypothesize that features like perceived power and control are essential for identifying an agent, while patients are picked out by movement at a human-like speed, having human-like facial features, and reacting to pain in a human-like way. A patient might also be identified because she is similar, familiar, or genetically related.

In a startling example of how genetic relatedness influences our moral judgments, the biologist April Bleske-Rechek and her colleagues (2010) used the trolley problem to modulate the relationship between the agent and people harmed, varying the victims by sex (M/F), age (2, 20, 45, 70), and relatedness (stranger, cousin, uncle/aunt, grandfather/grandmother, son/daughter, brother/sister, mother/father). Participants were then asked: "Would you flip the switch in this situation?"

The authors found that "participants were increasingly unwilling to flip the switch on targets of increasing levels of genetic relatedness." It won't surprise you that people are less willing to switch the track when it's their own mother on the side-track. What's surprising is the way that judgments appear to move *so* closely with genetic relatedness. While 77.4 percent of participants answered that they would flip the switch on a stranger, only 51.8 percent answered that they would flip the switch on a cousin (0.125 genetic relatedness), 47.4 percent answered that they would flip the switch on an aunt/uncle, nephew/niece, or grandparent (0.25 genetic relatedness), and 34.3 percent answered that they would flip the switch on a parent or sibling (0.5 genetic relatedness). Relying on genetic relatedness to identify moral importance can often lead to disastrous consequences; needless to say, if we are designing a machine based on our own moral judgments, this is not the kind of feature that will be helpful to incorporate.

Agents and patients are connected by the element CAUSE. In our original trolley scenario, most people judge switching the train onto a side-track to be morally permissible, but pushing a large man in front of the train as a means of stopping it to be morally wrong, even though they produce the same effects (one dead to save five). When my students are asked to explain what's different about these two scenarios, they often respond that pushing a man in front of a train is "actually killing him," while switching the train to a side-track is really just the train killing him. This sounds a bit strange at first. After all, murderers don't usually defend their action by insisting: "I didn't kill him, the bullet did!" One exception to this might be Charles Guiteau, who shot President James Garfield, inflicting what would have normally been a non-fatal wound, but one that the inept doctors treated with methods that led to Garfield's death. At trial, Guiteau famously insisted that he only shot Garfield, but the doctors had killed him. Cases like these bring in weird features of our perception of causation. It's true that Garfield wouldn't have died if not for Guiteau shooting him. But it's also true that other human agents (the doctors) played an important causal role in his death.

As psychologists who study causal reasoning have gradually discovered, there are many ways that people can think about causation. Sometimes this involves spatial processes like physical contact, but other times it involves thinking about what happens in alternate possibilities. In the physical-force kind, causation is a physical contact between entities where a quantity of the cause is transferred to a quantity in the effect. This is the difference between causing a man to die by pushing him versus directing a trolley in his direction. In the counterfactual kind of causal reasoning, causation is based on whether some outcome happens in alternate possibilities where the agent didn't intervene. When I say that Don Corleone caused the death of someone by ordering a hit, this doesn't necessarily require physical contact. All it requires is thinking about possibilities where Don Corleone didn't order the hit, and finding that the victim would have otherwise survived. Under the counterfactual interpretation, people are not only sensitive to whether harmful intentions actually cause harmful effects, but how *close* they come to doing so. Cases of negligence, victimless crimes, and attempted homicide are good examples.

Actions are more than just: AGENT CAUSE PATIENT. Instead, we care about a part of the agent's mind doing the work, and we can label that part of her mind with the category INTEND. Imagine the difference between seeing someone stumble and fall on a stranger, compared with the same person intentionally knocking the stranger down. Intention is the difference between murder and manslaughter, between harms done *accidentally* and *purposely*. Hurricanes and other natural disasters create more destruction than any serial killer, yet we don't view them as responsible for their actions because they don't have intentions. It's easy enough to recognize how important intentions are, but any lawyer will tell you that it's hard to establish when a person has one! We typically use cues like behavior, statements, and character traits to establish intent, but these aren't always reliable. Intention seems to be more than just a desire or motivation, and somehow connected to actual plans in a concrete way.

Intentions are not only important for agents, but also for determining which states are bad for patients. The concept of *consent* is produced when we consider the intentions of a patient. Specifically, when a patient intends to be in the state that the agent causes him to be in, that's probably what most speakers mean by an action being consensual. Actions like euthanasia, employment, and sex between willing partners are often different from murder, slavery, and rape entirely on the basis of consent. Just like verbal cues, behavior, and character are used to establish the intentions of the agent, the same kinds of evidence are often used to establish the consent of the patient. It should be noted that establishing a patient's consent is just as tricky as establishing an agent's intention, and many debates in ethics and law surround the conditions under which consent is or isn't present.

Finally, in addition to agents, patients, causes, and intentions, people are sensitive to an element that can be called HARM. The trolley problem is limited in that the same type of harm is always involved (physical harm). You might suspect that moral judgments often involve different types of harm, and you'd be correct. Some actions result in psychological and emotional damage, or destruction to people's reputation, social standing, or relationships. Lying, cheating, and stealing are often judged to be morally wrong, even if they don't necessarily involve direct physical harm. To give a physics analogy, the element HARM is more like a vector than a scalar: it doesn't just have a magnitude but also a *direction* in any number of possible dimensions of harm. If you thought that it was difficult to give precise conditions for what counts as an agent and a patient, or when intentions are present, you'll find it just as difficult to define and measure dimensions and magnitudes of harm.

The psychologist Jonathan Haidt (2012) denies that harm is an essential element in moral thinking, insisting that Western academics have narrowed the definition of morality to only those judgments involving harm but neglecting other important features of moral judgments like purity, authority, and sanctity. In my view, what we're calling HARM is not in conflict with disgust, since the two exist at different levels of explanation. HARM is an element in moral grammar used to measure the damage done to a patient; it can be instantiated by evaluations of physical suffering from a wide range of sources, including a projection of suffering from the evaluator's own disgust and purity judgments. This is where Hume was correct; people typically use their own emotional responses to evaluate harm. However, it's important that these emotions are also projected onto the agent, which is the difference between "that's gross" and "that's wrong." Experiments by Kurt Gray and colleagues (2014) suggest that even moral evaluations based on purity are always projected onto an implicit victim who suffers some damage. These victims might be people in alternate imagined realities, like the potential victims of drunk drivers or the potential children that might have existed from continuing a pregnancy. The patient is viewed as having a part of their identity damaged or destroyed, even if this entity is entirely a projection of the speaker's own emotional responses. Unfortunately, this is another inconsistent and inaccurate way humans apply moral rules that often leads to disastrous consequences.

Rules in moral grammar

If there's one rule that's consistent across the varieties of moral grammars, it's a rule against harmful battery. This is a point emphasized by John Mikhail (2014), who notes the consistencies across legal systems that define battery as: *an agent with a bad intention coming into contact with a non-consenting patient and producing bad consequences for that patient.* Representing this definition with our elements of moral grammar looks like the following:

Harmful battery

An agent's intention causes a patient to be in a state by **physical contact**, the state is **physically damaging** to the patient, and the patient doesn't intend to be in that state.[3]

There are three clauses in this definition (separated by *and*): one involving causation, the other involving harm, and the third involving consent. For instance, a criminal stabbing a random innocent person in the leg is an obvious case of battery, but a surgeon creating an incision in a patient's leg is *not* battery (even though it's causing the same state), because the patient has consented to the contact and it's not perceived as harm. The bystander who switches the train to a side-track causes the person on the side-track to be in a state of harm by pulling the switch, but this doesn't count as harmful battery, because it wasn't caused by direct physical force. You can already start to imagine all the possible variations of battery that can be generated by toggling the settings on these elements. Many of these are also established legal entities like "offensive battery," which toggles settings on the kinds of harm (physical vs. psychological):

Offensive battery

An agent's intention causes a patient to be in a state by **physical contact**, the state is **psychologically** distressing to the patient, and the patient doesn't intend to be in that state.[4]

We could also toggle the settings on CAUSE between physical contact and something more indirect, where an agent causes physical harm to the patient through *not* performing an action, which is called an omission. The agent performs an omission whenever she *could* have intervened in nearby counterfactual situations but doesn't, like allowing someone to drown when she could easily save them:

> **Harmful negligence**
>
> An agent's intention causes a patient to be in a state by **not** performing an action, the state is physically damaging to the patient, and the patient doesn't intend to be in that state.[5]

We won't get into the details about all these variations. I'll just note that they are much like the variations in natural languages: minor changes on a shared deep structure. We also won't worry too much about the exact structure of the concepts and rules. I agree with Mikhail that battery is a paradigm case of actions judged to be wrong, and that other wrong actions like homicide and rape can be generated by small variations in the actions defined here. It's also useful to show how this can generate the idea of an innocent person with respect to battery: a person is innocent of battery when they haven't intentionally caused it, even if they might still *intend* the patient to be in a bad state. Importantly, just *wanting* someone to experience harm might be permissible, but causing them to experience harm is wrong. As fictional detectives emphasize, there's nothing illegal about just wanting someone dead.

Under what conditions are actions like battery and homicide judged to be wrong? We could define a simple rule: "If [harmful battery], then wrong," but that's not enough to get at the complexities of people's beliefs. Almost everyone allows for battery in cases of punishment and self-defense. A more sophisticated rule that includes these cases would be a conditional that restricts the prohibition on battery to innocent people. Call this the *Intentional Harm Rule*:

> **Intentional Harm Rule**
>
> If an agent has not committed battery on you, then it's **not** permissible for you to commit battery on that agent.[6]

This rule essentially says: don't intentionally cause harm to innocent people without their consent. But our definition doesn't specify anything about guilty people, and we wanted to explain things like punishment and self-defense. Thus, we need to construct another rule within our system that accounts for the permissibility of retribution; call it the *Retribution Rule*:

> **Retribution Rule**
>
> If an agent has caused battery to you, then it is permissible to cause battery to that agent.[7]

The Retribution Rule can be toggled to form many varieties, like self-defense, revenge, and punishment. Despite the fact that the biblical Jesus claims that both punishment and revenge are impermissible, most Christians have historically ignored this teaching in their own moral judgments. This is yet another example of religious believers ignoring the commands of authorities about moral judgments.

Let's assume that these two rules, along with all the associated variations produced by toggling parameters, adequately explain human moral judgments. Following the linguistic analogy, we can think of these variations as different moral languages that are each derived from a set of universal elements.

Moral grammar machines

It's not hard to imagine using a combination of top-down and bottom-up approaches to turn our universal moral grammar into a computer program; each element has independently been successfully modeled. For decades, logicians and computer scientists have been developing deontic logic programs that can put into practice our intuitive reasoning about permissions and obligations. Wieringa and Meyer (2012) present a detailed overview of the ways in which deontic logic programs have been applied to domains like parking permits, tax law, and citizenship policies. The economist Susan Athey (2015) describes how machine learning techniques are currently being used to make extremely accurate causal predictions about the likely effects of administering a drug, merging two companies, or raising the price of a good. Categories like who counts as an AGENT or PATIENT can be easily modeled using a sufficiently large data set of human responses. However, the larger question that must be addressed when bringing these elements together into an artificial moral grammar is: *should* we be taking this approach to designing an ethical robot? Do we want robot ethics to be just another incarnation of our own moral judgments?

Consider a recent article from the journal *Cognition* titled "Learning a Commonsense Moral Theory" (2017), co-authored by Max Kleiman-Weiner, Rebecca Saxe, and Joshua Tenenbaum. In this article, the authors attempt to train a learning algorithm to develop something like the moral grammar described here. One component of their model is the evaluation of what I've been calling the PATIENT category. How will this system evaluate which people are valuable, and how much value is assigned to each person? The authors write:

> We start by supposing that through the course of one's life, one will acquire attachments for various people or even groups of people. These attachments and feelings can be represented through the vector introduced in the previous section. As mentioned in the introduction, these values could come from empathy and emotional responses, imagination and stories, morally charged analogical deliberation, love, contact, exposure etc.

In their artificial moral grammar, the organisms that a robot happens to engage with through contact, emotional bonding, and literature will become the ones that it finds to be valuable. But this is an arbitrary and limited method for determining what sorts of things are valuable. Asimov's laws were vague, but it's even worse to allow the details of what counts as a HARM and a PATIENT to be filled in by whatever the people around you happen to think. This will also inevitably lead to divergence and disagreement. Different machines will be exposed to different people, and thus form their own versions of our family and in-group preferences. Like it or not, it's necessary to make theoretical assumptions about what kind of information is relevant for these categories.

The other shortcoming of Asimov's laws also applies to our intuitive moral grammar: there is no way of deciding between two actions that both result in comparable levels of harm to equally valuable patients. Under the harmful battery rule, switching the track in the trolley problem is permissible, but under the negligence rule, it would be morally wrong, since you could easily save the person on the side-track. To resolve this conflict, we need to go beyond the level of how humans think about actions to how they *ought* to think.

The key to resolving these challenges will be identifying the *function* of moral grammar. If I want to know whether one machine is a better cash register than another machine, I can't just ask about its electronic wiring or the program it uses. Instead, I need to know what the *goal* of the system is: what is this machine designed to do? You tell me: "The function of a cash register is to identify items that are for sale, calculate their prices, and keep and exchange money." Now that I know what the machine is for, I can evaluate which machine is a *better* cash register. The same applies to our system of moral grammar. The next chapter will propose that there is an evolutionary and historical function behind our moral grammar. Understanding that function will give us a framework for determining which information we should use to fill in categories like PATIENT and HARM, as well as for unifying conflicting moral rules like the harmful battery rule and the negligence rule.

Chapter summary

- Moral judgments are probably distinct from related phenomena like emotional responses, social norms, and religious beliefs.
- Instead, moral judgments are the product of a psychological network of categories and rules, much like natural languages, that we can call "moral grammar."
- The universal categories in human moral grammar may be entities like: AGENT, PATIENT, INTEND, CAUSE, STATE, and HARM.
- These categories are structured to form complex moral concepts like *battery*, *innocence*, and *consent*, as well as rules like the Intentional Harm Rule and the Retribution Rule.
- A heterogeneous set of psychological mechanisms are used to sort objects into these abstract categories. For instance, mechanisms for identifying genetic

relatedness, familiarity, and empathy may be used to identify who counts as a PATIENT. Events may be linked together by CAUSE through more statistical inferences or more abstract, counterfactual inferences. States that count as HARM may be very dependent on an individual's emotional responses and cultural norms.

- Many situations exist where every action results in perceived harm to some patient, leading to undecidability in moral grammar.
- Top-down approaches can be used to model our intuitive moral grammar, and bottom-up approaches can be used to simulate the psychological mechanisms that apply it. However, these algorithms will incorporate all of the problems of arbitrariness, conflicting mechanisms, and undecidability. To resolve this, a framework is needed to enable the successful features of moral grammar to be preserved and the unfortunate ones to be discarded.

Notes

1 For those readers who have taken an introductory logic course, you recognize the inferences with *all* and *some* as quantifier negation and quantifier entailment, where for some well-formed formula A:

1. $\forall A \equiv \neg \exists \neg A$
2. $\neg \forall A \equiv \exists \neg A$
3. $\forall A \Rightarrow \exists A$

The inferences with *must* and *acceptable* are structurally identical versions with the obligatory (O) and permissible (P) operators:

1. $O(A) \equiv \neg P(\neg A)$
2. $\neg O(A) \equiv P(\neg A)$
3. $O(A) \Rightarrow P(A)$

2 If terms like *wrong* and *permissible* are quantifiers that take propositions as input, then we should expect their input to have the component parts of propositions. In modern logic, propositions are composed of predicates and Boolean operators. Predicates are functions that take objects as input and produce truth-values (T/F, or 1/0) as outputs. For example, a predicate like HAPPY (__) means "__ is happy," and TALLER (__,__), means "__ is taller than __." Putting information in the blank slots will produce an output of true/1 or false/0. For instance, if Sean is happy, then HAPPY (Sean) will map to True/1. Boolean operators (and, or, not, if-then) take truth-values as input and generate truth-values as outputs. In this framework, we can represent moral rules as composed of quantifications over predicates and Boolean operators. The "features" I've listed are really predicate functions that look like the following:

AGENT(_)
PATIENT(_)
INTEND(_,_)
CAUSE(_,_)
STATE(_,_)
HARM(_,_)

3 Being precise, a definition of harmful battery might be contained within the scope of existential quantifiers:

$\exists(x)\exists(y)\exists(z)$
$[\text{AGENT}(x) \& \text{PATIENT}(y) \& \text{STATE}(y,z)$
$\& \text{CAUSE}_{\text{Contact}}(\text{INTEND}(x,\text{STATE}(y,z)))$
$\& \text{HARM}_{\text{Physical}}(y,z)$
$\& \neg \text{INTEND}(y,\text{STATE}(y,z)))]$

4 Formally:

$\exists(x)\exists(y)\exists(z)$
$[\text{AGENT}(x) \& \text{PATIENT}(y) \& \text{STATE}(y,z)$
$\& \text{CAUSE}_{\text{Contact}}(\text{INTEND}(x,\text{STATE}(y,z)))$
$\& \text{HARM}_{\text{Psychological}}(y,z)$
$\& \neg \text{INTEND}(y,\text{STATE}(y,z)))]$

5 Formally:

$\exists(x)\exists(y)\exists(z)$
$[\text{AGENT}(x) \& \text{PATIENT}(y) \& \text{STATE}(y,z)$
$\& \text{CAUSE}_{\text{Omission}}(\text{INTEND}(x,\text{STATE}(y,z)))$
$\& \text{HARM}_{\text{Physical}}(y,z)$
$\& \neg \text{INTEND}(y,\text{STATE}(y,z)))]$

6 If [not] HARMFUL BATTERY (*x,y*), then [wrong] HARMFUL BATTERY (*y,x*)
7 If HARMFUL BATTERY (*x,y*), then [permissible] HARMFUL BATTERY (*y,x*)

References

Athey, Susan (2015). "Beyond Prediction: Using Big Data for Policy Problems." *Science*, 335, 483–385.
Ayer, Alfred Jules (1936). *Language, Truth, and Logic*. London: Gollancz Press.
Bleske-Rechek, April & Nelson, Lyndsay & Baker, Jonathan & Remiker, Mark & Brandt, Sarah (2010). "Evolution and the Trolley Problem: People Save Five over One Unless the One Is Young, Genetically Related, or a Romantic Partner." *Journal of Social, Evolutionary, and Cultural Psychology*, 4, 115–127.
Brown, Donald (1991). *Human Universals*. New York: McGraw-Hill.
Cushman, Fiery & Greene, Joshua (2012). "Finding Faults: How Moral Dilemmas Illuminate Cognitive Structure." *Social Neuroscience*, 7, 269–279.
Foot, Philippa (1967). "The Problem of Abortion and the Doctrine of the Double Effect." *Oxford Review*, 5, 5–15.

Gray, Kurt & Schein, Chelsea & Ward, Adrian (2014). "The Myth of Harmless Wrongs." *The Journal of Experimental Psychology*, 143, 1600–1615.

Haidt, Jonathan (2012). *The Righteous Mind*. New York: Pantheon.

Hume, David (1738). *A Treatise of Human Nature*. Oxford: Oxford University Press.

Kant, Immanuel (1798). *The Conflict of the Faculties*. Trans. Mary J. Gregor. Lincoln, NE: University of Nebraska Press.

Kleiman-Weiner, Max & Saxe, Rebecca & Tenenbaum, Joshua (2017). "Learning a Commonsense Moral Theory." *Cognition*, 167, 107–123.

Kratzer, Angelika (1977). "What 'Must' and 'Can' Must and Can Mean." *Linguistics and Philosophy*, 1, 337–355.

Marr, David (1981). *Vision*. San Francisco, CA: Freeman Press.

Mikhail, John (2011). *Elements of Moral Cognition: Rawls's Linguistic Analogy and the Cognitive Science of Moral and Legal Judgment*. Cambridge: Cambridge University Press.

Mikhail, John (2014). "Any Animal Whatever? Harmful Battery and Its Elements as Building Blocks of Moral Cognition." *Ethics*, 124, 750–786.

Plato (c. 380 BC). *The Republic*. Trans. R.E. Allen (2006). New Haven, CT: Yale University Press.

Rachels, James (2009). "The Challenge of Cultural Relativism." In: Steven M. Cahn (ed.) *Exploring Philosophy*. Oxford: Oxford University Press.

Thomson, Judith (1976). "Killing, Letting Die, and the Trolley Problem." *The Monist*, 59, 204–217.

Turiel, Elliot (1983). *The Development of Social Knowledge: Morality and Convention*. Cambridge: Cambridge University Press.

Wegner, Daniel & Gray, Kurt (2016). *The Mind Club: Who Thinks, What Feels, and Why It Matters*. New York: Penguin Press.

Wieringa, Roel & Meyer, John-Jules. (2012). "Applications of Deontic Logic in Computer Science: A concise overview." In: Roel Wieringa & John-Jules Meyer (eds.) *Deontic Logic in Computer Science: Normative System Specification*. New York: John Wiley & Sons.

2
COOPERATION PROBLEMS

The *HMS Beagle* arrived in the Galapagos Islands in September 1835, almost four years into its journey around the world. The young naturalist, Charles Darwin, departed the ship and immediately set to work collecting specimens with the help of his servant, Syms Covington. Some of these included the famous Galapagos finches, although Darwin didn't seem to pay much attention to them at the time. When they returned to England and presented the finches to the Zoological Society of London, Darwin was surprised when the ornithologist John Gould reported that the finches he collected were not just one finch but a *dozen* previously undiscovered species of finches. One of the most notable differences between these species is the size and shape of their beaks; the finches on one island have long and thin beaks, while the finches on another island have short and strong beaks. What fascinated Darwin was the connection between these different beaks and the environment on each island. On the island with seeds as the most obvious source of food, the finches have strong beaks that seem tailor-made for crushing shells. On the island where insects inside of small spaces are the obvious source of food, the finches have long and thin beaks. In his published journals, now called *The Voyage of the Beagle* (1845), Darwin subtly entertained a hypothesis about this observation: "one might really fancy that from an original paucity of birds in this archipelago, one species had been taken and modified for different ends."

Darwin's finches have been used as the paradigmatic case of evolutionary adaptations, and Darwin himself spent years researching pigeon breeding. It seems like bird-watching lends itself to thinking about evolution. In fact, Darwin's friend Charles Lyell recommended formulating his theory of evolution within a book entirely about pigeons ("everybody loves pigeons," he wrote to Darwin). On an episode of my favorite podcast, the BBC radio program *In Our Time*, biologist Steve Jones confessed:

> I often think that all biologists ... have a guilty secret, which is that they started as bird-watchers. I started as a bird-watcher. I filled the little ticks in

my book, and it never crossed my mind to ask: "Why do ducks have very bright colored males, and females are rather brown, whereas in swans the genders look much the same?"

For a long time, it was thought that asking *why*-questions in biology doesn't make sense. Why do finches on this island have long and thin beaks, while finches on the other island have short and strong beaks? Maybe science just can't answer questions like this, or maybe the answer is that God gave them traits to match their environment. In his *Origin of Species* (1859), Darwin proposed another possibility: natural selection. Natural selection is a simple process that operates whenever there are three conditions present: (1) there is random mutation in traits, (2) some traits cause greater rates of reproduction than others, (3) these traits are heritable (Nowak, 2006). Darwin's idea was that an original species of finch historically spread onto many different islands in the Galapagos. There is always some degree of random variation in the sizes of beaks, and on the island with plenty of seeds, the birds with beaks better at crushing shells get more food, leading them to reproduce more. Because these traits are heritable, their offspring also have the strong beaks of their parents, so they continue reproducing at a higher rate. Eventually, the trait of strong beaks spreads throughout the population on the seed island. This process has been described by Richard Dawkins (1986) as a blind watchmaker: traits are selected because of the benefits in survival and reproduction that they provide, but the traits themselves are produced by chance mutations rather than intentional design. Biological traits produced by this invisible hand are called *adaptations*.

Throughout most of the twentieth century, only physical traits like thumbs and hearts were viewed as the products of natural selection. Towards the end of the century, many biologists and psychologists began to think about emotions and cognitive traits like language, memory, and reasoning as products of natural selection as well. It's one thing to study a physical trait like beak size as the product of natural selection. But it's another to study a *behavior* as the product of natural selection. What would evidence for this even look like? Yet again, bird-watching provides an answer. In the 1970s, a group of biologists led by John Krebs used a method for explaining foraging behavior in birds called *optimality modeling*, which has become a primary tool of behavioral ecologists (Krebs et al., 1977). This method aims at giving a formal model for the solution to a problem, and then testing these models against behaviors. If behavior matches the model, then the best explanation for this match is that the organism has adapted specifically in response to that problem. To show that foraging behavior is an evolutionary adaptation, Krebs and his colleagues first identified the goal of the behavior: gathering as much food as possible while spending as little energy as possible. The researchers then developed a set of equations that describe the optimal strategy for foraging based on factors like the energy gained from prey, the energy spent to obtain it, and the rate at which these types of prey are encountered. Krebs and colleagues then set out to test these equations against the actual foraging behavior of birds like the great titmouse. In laboratory conditions where they manipulated the size of prey, the time and energy it took to catch them, and the rate at which they were encountered, Krebs found a surprising match between the predictions of their model and the animal's actual behavior.

This chapter proposes that our moral grammar, just like the beaks of the Galapagos finches and the foraging behavior of the great titmouse, is an adaptation produced by either natural or cultural selection processes. I'm being careful to say "evolutionary *or* cultural processes," because there are also cultural processes that can produce adaptive behavior, and it's often difficult to distinguish from biological selection. The analogy between natural and cultural selection was popularized by Richard Dawkins in his book, *The Selfish Gene* (1976), where he suggested that ideas often act like genes (to describe this analogy, he coined the word *meme*). If ideas have variation, an effect on the success of an organism, and can be replicated by others with high fidelity, then a Darwinian selection for ideas can occur within human cultures. The analogy between cultural and natural selection isn't perfect, but we can ignore most of the problems here. I'm officially neutral about whether moral grammar is the product of nature, culture, or both. The only point I wish to make is that there is *some* practical function causally responsible for our moral grammar. Viewing moral grammar as an adaptation is extremely important, because understanding the selection pressures that guided its evolution can help us to *evaluate moral theories*.

This is a conclusion that Darwin himself came to about moral judgments. In *Descent of Man* (1871), he conjectured that moral thinking "first developed, in order that those animals which would profit by living in society, should be induced to live together." Let's call this the Evolutionary Hypothesis:

> **Evolutionary Hypothesis:** Moral judgments are the product of evolutionary pressures for cooperative behavior in self-interested organisms.

This hypothesis is extremely popular among moral psychologists of very different theoretical backgrounds. At the 2017 meeting of the Moral Psychology Research Group, I conducted an informal poll during my talk, and found that the entire audience (except one notable holdout) agreed with this hypothesis. To lend support to the evolutionary hypothesis, this chapter will present an optimality modeling argument, similar to the one presented by Krebs and his colleagues about foraging behaviors in the great titmouse. We'll start with an evolutionary problem, model the optimal solutions, and then compare these results to the rules in our own moral grammar. It turns out that computer programs have been quite useful in modeling optimal solutions to this problem, but they often get stuck in "local minima" or fail to generalize to noncooperative situations, and a moral theory is needed to break out of these inevitable traps.

The problem of cooperation

Do humans act purely out of self-interest? The annoying (but true) response to this question is: it depends on how you define "self-interest." If you define it narrowly to mean those actions that a person believes will increase her wealth or pleasure, then the answer is obviously "no." People regularly volunteer at homeless shelters, give to charity, and sometimes even jump in front of subway trains to rescue complete strangers. On the other hand, if you define "self-interest" broadly enough to mean "anything that a person prefers," then the answer is obviously (and trivially) "yes." If someone volunteers at a homeless shelter, it's because she prefers doing that to staying at home and watching cat videos. This broader definition of self-interest is what I have in mind. In this sense, it's trivially true that agents always act to maximize their preferences. If a man gives away all his money, it means he prefers to be poor rather than rich. If a woman kills herself, it means she preferred to die rather than to live. All of these actions are "self-interested" in this very trivial sense.

There are some social interactions where my interests are the opposite of yours. For instance, if we're playing a game of chess or fighting a war, the outcomes that are very good for me are very bad for you, and vice versa. These are *zero-sum games*, since my gains all come at the expense of your losses. However, there are other social interactions, like friendship, where outcomes can be mutually beneficial. Both of us are lonely on Saturday night, and we enjoy each other's company, so it benefits us both to watch a movie together. Economists often call these *cooperative* interactions, and there is a sense in which that's correct. Most dictionary definitions of "cooperation" require only two or more people who are "working together for mutual benefit." But the problem that Darwin and others propose as the historical catalyst for moral thinking is more specific than this, since self-interest alone is enough to get people to work together for mutual benefit. For example, consider two friends who love skydiving together, David and Tamler. Imagine that they most prefer skydiving together, but still enjoy going on their own and watching other people skydive. Let's rank their preferences, from highest (3) to lowest (0):

3: Jump together
2: Jump alone
1: Watch the other person jump
0: Nobody jumps.

Since each player only has two options (jump or don't jump), we can represent all the outcomes within a 2-by-2 matrix in Figure 2.1.[1]

The numbers in each box represent preferences as: (David's preference, Tamler's preference), so an outcome of (1, 2) is ranked 1 by David and ranked 2 by Tamler. Once we represent the situation in this way, there are several tools from the field known as game theory that can help to determine which action is in the self-interest of each player. Game theory *does* apply to traditional games like chess and poker, but it also applies to war, politics, relationships, business, and any situation where at least two people are interacting in a way where their decisions influence the other player's outcomes. The most famous solution to games like this skydiving game was developed by the Nobel laureate John Nash (whose struggles with schizophrenia were the subject of *A Beautiful Mind*). According to Nash, the best strategy for a player to use is one where she can't

Skydiving Game

Tamler

	Jump	Stay
David Jump	<u>3</u>, <u>3</u>	<u>2</u>, 1
David Stay	1, <u>2</u>	0, 0

FIGURE 2.1 Two friends with preferences ranked: jump together (3), jump alone (2), watch the other person jump (1), nobody jumps (0). The best responses to the other player's actions are underlined, with the Nash Equilibrium point being (Jump, Jump).

improve her payoffs when other players are also playing their best strategies. A "Nash Equilibrium" is a point where no player can improve her payoffs when all other players are also playing their best strategies.[2] We won't worry about the formal details here, but there is an easy way to find these points in a matrix like Figure 2.1: underline the best payoffs for David in each of Tamler's actions, and then underline the best payoffs for Tamler in each of David's actions. If there's an outcome where all the payoffs are underlined, it's a Nash Equilibrium.

You don't have to do the math in order to figure out that it's in both David's and Tamler's mutual interests to jump together. This is a case where both players, acting purely out of self-interest, will also produce an outcome which maximizes their mutual benefit. However, the social problems that Darwin and others have in mind are ones where pure self-interest *fails* to produce mutual benefit.

A cooperation problem is a situation where selfish actions lead to outcomes where *all players* would have preferred a different result. To get an idea of this problem, consider a story about two grain farmers described by David Hume (1738):

> Your corn is ripe today; mine will be so tomorrow.' Tis profitable for us both, that I should labour with you today, and that you should aid me tomorrow. I have no kindness for you, and know you have as little for me. I will not, therefore, take any pains on your account; and should I labour with you upon my own account, in expectation of a return, I know I should be disappointed, and that I should in vain depend upon your gratitude. Here then I leave you to labour alone: You treat me in the same manner. The seasons change; and both of us lose our harvests for want of mutual confidence and security.

The two farmers in Hume's story know that cooperating will produce a better outcome for both. However, with cooperation, there is always the possibility

30 Cooperation problems

that the other player will take advantage of your help and not offer any in return. Because each farmer is worried about being exploited, neither offers assistance and, consequently, both lose the mutual benefits. Situations like this are common in trade, production of food, mating, and war. More food per person can be produced by agriculture than by hunting and gathering, but agriculture requires cooperation and storage which can be taken advantage of by thieves. Loaning money can be beneficial to both parties, but the lender always risks someone running off with her money. Two villages may gain strength by forming an alliance, but by letting their guards down, each runs the risk of its ally taking over.

To model the problem of cooperation as a game, we can construct a simultaneous two-player game where each player prefers mutual cooperation to mutual defection, while at the same time preferring most to successfully take advantage of their partner, and preferring least to be taken advantage of. This game is known as the *Prisoner's Dilemma*. Using the conventions of game theory, the Prisoner's Dilemma is set up as a matrix with two players, where each player has two possible moves: cooperate or defect. Let's call the two hypothetical players in this game Sean and Ethan, and we can imagine them as the grain farmers from Hume's story. Each player's preference is represented with an ordinal number, where higher ordinal numbers represent higher preferences. Listing out each outcome from least favorite (0) to most favorite (3):

0: Being exploited
1: Mutual defection
2: Mutual cooperation
3. Exploiting the other player.

Once again, we can represent all the outcomes within a 2-by-2 matrix like Figure 2.2.

Prisoner's Dilemma

Sean

	C	D
C	2, 2	0, 3
D	3, 0	1, 1

Ethan

FIGURE 2.2 Payoffs in Prisoner's Dilemma, where C = Cooperate and D = Defect. The numbers are ordered: (Ethan's Payoff, Sean's Payoff), so when Ethan cooperates and Sean defects, that is ranked 0 for Ethan and 3 for Sean.

If you were playing this game, which move gets you the most rewards? It turns out there is only one Nash Equilibrium for this game, and it is for both players to defect. In fact, you don't even need to use this tool, since just about any measurement of self-interest will tell you that defecting is the best choice here (for that reason, defecting is called a *strictly dominating* strategy). If you are Sean, you don't know what Ethan is going to do. But you *do* know that if Ethan cooperates, then defecting will get you a payoff of 3 rather than 2. You also know that if Ethan defects, then defecting will get you a payoff of 1 rather than 0. Same goes for Ethan. This suggests that cheating in situations like these is the rational choice for all players.

This result is shocking. Unlike in the skydiving game, both players acting in their self-interest produces a result where both would *prefer a different outcome* (Sean and Ethan both prefer mutual cooperation over mutual defection). Whenever there is an outcome which would be an improvement for at least one player without making another one worse-off, this is called a Pareto-improvement, named after the Italian economist and engineer Vilfredo Pareto.[3] For example, throwing away the rest of your dinner while I am sitting next to you starving to death would be Pareto-inefficient. Giving me your food would be a Pareto-improvement on the current state, since it would make me much better-off, without making you any worse-off. It's the fact that this standard solution to the Prisoner's Dilemma game is *not Pareto-optimal* that has historically caused people to tear out their hair in frustration. In fact, we can go even further: the Nash Equilibrium has an outcome that is a universal Pareto-improvement, meaning that *all* the players prefer the box with (2,2) over the box with (1,1). Still, somehow both act in a way that they know will produce (1,1).[4] This is the problem that social contract theorists have focused on: where points that are produced by self-interest (Nash Equilibria) have alternatives that all players would prefer (universal Pareto-improvements). Here, what we can call "cooperative behavior" always involves both players risking some potential loss or sacrificing some potential gain to reach that Pareto-improvement point.

According to this definition of a cooperation problem, the Prisoner's Dilemma is the strongest example of a cooperation game. However, there are plenty of situations which are "weaker" versions of the cooperation problem. One example is a game called Stag Hunt, which comes from a story told by Jean-Jacques Rousseau (1762) about two hunters who could decide to either cooperate and hunt a stag for a larger mutual payoff, or defect and decide to hunt a hare for a lesser (but still acceptable) dinner. The philosopher Brian Skyrms (1996) has argued that Stag Hunt models many of the important features of social cooperation better than Prisoner's Dilemma. Capturing a stag requires two hunters, so cooperating still introduces vulnerability. However, in this case (as opposed to Prisoner's Dilemma), the other player doesn't have as much incentive to cheat, since a hare dinner could just as well be obtained from both players defecting. Let's say that both players most prefer hunting a stag together, and least prefer to be hunting a stag alone. The other remaining options are intermediate in

32 Cooperation problems

Stag Hunt

	Sean C	Sean D
Ethan C	2, 2	0, 1
Ethan D	1, 0	1, 1

FIGURE 2.3 Payoffs in Stag Hunt, which are similar to the payoffs in Prisoner's Dilemma, but without any incentive for exploitation.

preference, but neither is preferred. Figure 2.3 shows both players' preferences for each outcome.

In Stag Hunt, both players can decide between a guaranteed medium payoff by defecting, or a sort of *double or nothing* option, which is riskier. This is a bit like if someone offers you either a 100 percent chance of ten dollars, versus a 50/50 chance of 20 dollars or nothing. Deciding to cooperate is a riskier strategy, but it's mathematically identical to defecting. As opposed to the Prisoner's Dilemma, there are two pure Nash Equilibria for this game, (2, 2) and (1, 1), and one mixed (or probabilistic) equilibrium of flipping a coin between the two choices. This produces the same Pareto-optimality problem as with Prisoner's Dilemma, where half the time people will follow strategies that lead to outcomes where both players are worse off.

Machines playing cooperation games

The well-defined structure of Prisoner's Dilemma raises the enticing prospect of designing computer programs that play against each other in iterated versions of the game. In the past 40 years, there have been literally thousands of published papers which have done exactly that. The earliest competition between computer programs playing Prisoner's Dilemma games was held by the political scientist Robert Axelrod in 1979. Mathematicians and economists were invited to submit computer algorithms which would compete in round-robin Prisoner's Dilemma games. The results were described in Axelrod's book, *The Evolution of Cooperation* (1984). The two simplest pure strategies are to always defect no matter what (Hawk), or always cooperate no matter what (Dove). These can be represented as a single state that the program moves into which will always return to the same state, regardless of what the other player's move is (*C* or *D*). These two strategies are illustrated in Figure 2.4.

The initial arrow represents the first move, which sets the program into its initial state. The looping arrow represents every subsequent move, which sends

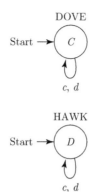

FIGURE 2.4 Dove and Hawk Strategies in Repeated Prisoner's Dilemma. Dove = always cooperate, Hawk = always defect.

the program into the same state no matter what the other player does (the other player's moves are indicated by the lower-case letters *c* and *d*). If you don't understand these diagrams, you can ignore them and just focus on the descriptions.

More complicated strategies can be represented by two-state diagrams. One of them, called Grim Trigger, was submitted to Axelrod's tournament by the economist James Friedman. Essentially, this strategy plays Dove until the other player defects, then it switches permanently to Hawk (Figure 2.5). The two states of the program are thus C and defect D; the program starts in C and only shifts to D when the opposing player defects.

In Axelrod's tournament, the algorithms played against each other in multiple rounds of Prisoner's Dilemma games, with the winning algorithm being the one to achieve the highest overall score. For example, a Dove program playing against another Dove program would consistently get a payoff of 2, since both programs always cooperate. However, a Dove program playing against a Hawk program would consistently get 0, since it would keep cooperating while the other player keeps defecting. A Hawk playing against Grim would initially get 3, but then only 1 on all subsequent rounds, once Grim has switched over to always defecting.

Axelrod found that the winning algorithm in his tournaments was the two-state program called Tit-for-Tat, which starts out like Grim, but it will switch

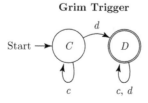

FIGURE 2.5 Grim Trigger Strategy in Repeated Prisoner's Dilemma. Cooperate initially, and then keep cooperating as long as the other player cooperates. As soon as the other player defects, switch to always defect.

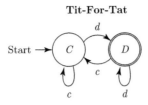

FIGURE 2.6 Tit-for-Tat Strategy in Repeated Prisoner's Dilemma. Cooperate on the first move, then do whatever the other player did on her previous move. If the other player cooperates, you cooperate. If the other player defects, you defect.

back to Dove when the opponent starts to cooperate again. Tit-for-Tat is pleasantly simple; it essentially starts out cooperating and then just mimics whatever the other player's previous move was (Figure 2.6).

Axelrod praised Tit-for-Tat's virtues as being *nice, not envious, quick to punish*, and *quick to forgive*.[5] A strategy is nice when its first state is cooperation. In this sense, Grim and Dove are nice strategies, while Hawk isn't. Not being envious means it accepts getting a payoff of 2 without trying to get 3. Other programs might randomly defect just to see if the other player is playing Dove. However, Tit-for-Tat is content with always cooperating so long as the other player cooperates, even if the other player turns out to be playing Dove. Being *quick to punish* and *quick to forgive* means that the program immediately goes into a defect state to punish defection, but immediately returns to a cooperative state once the other player cooperates. Another important virtue of Tit-for-Tat is that it's simple. All these strategies are pure (as opposed to mixed) strategies, which follow deterministic rules that are easy for other players to identify and predict. It's also less expensive for an organism to play Tit-for-Tat, since it doesn't need to perform any complicated statistical techniques over large amounts of data. Instead, all players need to do in Tit-for-Tat is keep track of the last move of the player they're currently interacting with.

There is one important problem with the strategy: Tit-for-Tat can't tell the difference between genuine defections and simple errors. If one of the other players defects by accident, this will send two players both using Tit-for-Tat into a "death spiral" from which neither ever emerges. However, various methods have been developed for equipping Tit-for-Tat with some way to distinguish genuine from accidental defections, like requiring two defections from the other player, a program called Tit-for-Two-Tats.

During the years since Axelrod's original tournament, hundreds of new programs were developed for playing Prisoner's Dilemma games, and a new tournament was organized by the Institute of Electrical and Electronics Engineers (IEEE) in 2004. Over 223 programs were entered, but as noted in a 2012 review paper, the winning algorithms all built on the basic features in Tit-for-Tat that were originally praise by Axelrod:

> [B]asic rules for cooperation that were recognized by Axelrod in the first competition are still valid: kindness, provocability, forgiveness and

simplicity. Most of new successful strategies are based on principles that were set up 20 or 30 years ago (from 223 strategies at the competition 1 in the year 2004 there were 73 based on TFT principle).

(Jurisic et al., 2012)

A reasonable conclusion is that strategies with features like Tit-for-Tat are the optimal ones in cooperation games like Prisoner's Dilemma.

At this point, we might ask ourselves the same question reached at the end of the previous chapter: should we design ethical robots based on successful algorithms in cooperation problems? Just like a system modeled after our intuitive moral grammar, it would be a good start, but there are serious limitations. Working to solve this problem from the bottom-up can cause a system to get stuck in "local maxima," which are "good enough" solutions to the problem. For example, in Peter Danielson's book, *Artificial Morality* (1992), he describes simulations of iterated Prisoner's Dilemma games with computer programs that interacted with each other over long periods of time. In Danielson's simulations, there emerged distinct "tribes" of cooperators separating from "tribes" of defectors, wars between the tribes, the emergence of occasional criminals within cooperative groups, and so on. The point here isn't that this is optimal behavior, it's that satisfying behavior that is *seriously flawed but still good enough* emerges from a bottom-up approach.

Another important limitation of Tit-for-Tat is that it doesn't generalize to *non-cooperative* situations where cooperating with one player means defecting with another. Trolley-style dilemmas are the obvious examples, where saving one person's life means allowing the other person to die. What does Tit-for-Tat tell us to do in this scenario? The answer is nothing, since there is no way to cooperate with a cooperator without, at the same time, defecting with a cooperator. For this reason, Tit-for-Tat might be a special case of a more general cooperation rule that will *reduce* to it in the appropriate context. If this were true, we could use the same general principle for producing cooperative behavior in both cooperative *and* non-cooperative situations. The next chapter will argue that this is the goal of a moral theory. But first, I'll need to say more about why morality and cooperation are linked together.

Morality is cooperation

I was once having a conversation with an evolutionary psychologist, and when I told him that I worked on ethics, he responded: "I don't think that morality exists." I was surprised, and asked him if he never judges any actions to be wrong. He replied that these responses are "nothing more than the product of adapted mechanisms for social cooperation." I thought this was funny, because my view is that moral rules *are* adaptive solutions to cooperation problems. "Oh," he said with a shrug, "if *that's* what you mean by morality, then sure."

Lacking shared definitions is a problem in any important debate. If we don't mean the same thing by words like *God*, *socialism*, or *morality*, then we're just talking past each other. People debating about the existence of God often have very different definitions. An atheist says: "Why would an all-good and all-powerful being allow children to get cancer?" The theist, with a confused expression, responds: "But I don't think God is all-good or all-powerful, I think he is the ground of all being [or whatever]." Just like my friend, the atheist shrugs and says: "Oh, well, if that's what you mean by God, then maybe that exists, but I don't care about that." How do we deal with this problem of definitions? One easy way is to just have people define what they mean from the beginning of a debate. But sometimes people aren't good at defining what they mean, and sometimes *they're* even mistaken about what they're talking about. For instance, if a theist says that the word *God* doesn't have any connection to having a mind or being all-powerful and all-good, this contradicts the way that most people use the word in everyday life. Why would anyone pray to a being that doesn't have a mind or the power to change your circumstances? So now I face the same challenge: if I am saying that *morality* refers to optimal strategies for cooperation problems, how do I show that this is what other people mean by that word, and not just a weird definition of mine?[6]

One way to link together moral grammar and cooperative strategies is with an optimality modeling argument. Krebs and his colleagues found that their predictions for optimal foraging behavior nicely matched the actual foraging behavior that birds display in the lab. I want to show that optimal solutions to cooperation problems, like Tit-For-Tat, have a structural identity to the rules that we observe in our intuitive moral grammar. Consider the rules in moral grammar from the previous chapter:

Intentional Harm Rule:

If [not] HARMFUL BATTERY (x,y), then
[not permissible] HARMFUL BATTERY (y,x)

Retribution Rule:

If HARMFUL BATTERY (x,y), then
[permissible] HARMFUL BATTERY (y,x)

Now compare these to the rules in Tit-For-Tat:

Cooperate with Cooperators:

If [not] DEFECT (x,y), then
[move to] COOPERATE (y,x)

Defect with Defectors:

If DEFECT (x,y), then
[move to] DEFECT (y,x)

The correspondence between these rules should be clear. This structural identity would be extremely unlikely if cooperation problems played no role in the causal history of moral judgments. Therefore, the best explanation for this connection is that moral judgments are adaptations to solve the problem of cooperation. As it stands, this is by no means a knock-down argument for the evolutionary hypothesis. One might object that a structural correspondence is likely to exist at any level of generality between two systems. But it's an argument that can be supplemented with further evidence from the growing field studying the evolution of moral judgments.

The rules in moral grammar might be thought of as an interesting variation on Tit-for-Tat strategies, something like *Tit for Intentional Tat*. We saw how the original Tit-for-Tat strategy can't distinguish intentional defections from accidental ones, and because of this, it has the potential of sliding into a death spiral between both players. One solution to this problem is to have some method for evaluating whether the defection was intentional. This definition also matches our expectations that morality is an objective, mind-independent set of rules that are distinct from social conventions, religious commands, and emotional reactions. Good strategies are objective and mind-independent objects that are good for you regardless of whether you agree with them. It's certainly true that optimal strategies are *about* preferences, but their optimality doesn't *depend on* preferences. This is just to say that optimality, just like morality, is completely independent of what people think or how they feel.

You might object that strategies in cooperation games are connected to *self-interest* in a way that morality shouldn't be. It only makes sense to talk about Tit-for-Tat being the optimal strategy in relation to the goal of maximizing self-interest. But isn't morality supposed to be completely independent of self-interest? According to my view, if a player is guaranteed the ability to permanently exploit the other player, then she should immediately throw morality out the window. But philosophers have emphasized how morality gives people reasons to cooperate, even when it isn't in their self-interest at all. To illustrate this, let's create a game called the Exploitation Game, where the payoffs are the same as a cooperation game, but Player A is in a position to force Player B to always cooperate, leaving him free to always defect. This is an idealized master-slave scenario, where there's no possibility of a slave uprising; the master is guaranteed to always be in a position to exploit the slave.

In ethics, this is called the problem of *amoralism*, and was originally raised by Plato in the opening pages of the *Republic*. Plato describes the story of a man who has power to exploit anybody without consequences. The man is a farmer named Gyges, who discovers a magical ring that gives him invisibility. Now that Gyges has the power to do whatever he wants without any punishment, he immediately begins a crime spree. Gyges is an amoralist, someone who doesn't care about morality because he can do what he wants without fear of punishment. The challenge here is to offer some argument for why Gyges should refrain from harming others, even when it's in his interest to harm them, and he can get away with it. Plato spends the rest of the dialogue trying to do this, but there has been long historical disagreement about whether this challenge can be met. Thomas Hobbes (1651) and David Gauthier (1986) accept that there *is no* response to Plato's challenge.

If morality is a strategy that players adopt for the purpose of maximizing their long-term interests, then it no longer applies once long-term interests can be improved more by force than by cooperation. I think that this is partly correct; morality stops being practically valuable to someone who has the chance to permanently play the Exploitation Game. However, it's not true that moral rules simply cease to exist or no longer apply to this person. Slavery and exploitation are *still* cooperation games, because the payoffs remain essentially the same for both players. And so long as it's still a cooperation game, morality as a strategy for cooperation games still applies. Gyges is playing Hawk, which is uncooperative behavior *by definition*, so it's still morally wrong. Thus, Gyges is doing something wrong, even if he has no practical reason to care about doing the right thing.

Strategies, in my view, are abstract objects that exist whether or not they are valuable to anybody. Take a chess strategy like *Queen's Gambit*. Sometimes this is in the interest of a player, and sometimes it's not. Even when it's not in a player's interests to use it, the strategy still *exists*, as an abstract entity that emerges from the facts about the game of chess. It doesn't just go away because people aren't playing it. I won't dwell too much on where this position fits in amongst the many meta-ethical positions developed by philosophers, except that it is a genuine form of moral realism (called *moral naturalism*).[7] Anti-realists are partially correct that moral claims emerge from human activities and fundamentally involve our interests, but anti-realists are mistaken that moral claims can't be true independently of our beliefs and other attitudes. It still makes sense to say: "According to Queen's Gambit, you ought to make this move," even when there's no practical value in using Queen's Gambit, or the players have no knowledge or interest in the strategy. A chess player may also reply: "I don't care." Since morality is a strategy that emerges from cooperation games, then so long as someone is playing a cooperation game, the strategy still exists, whether or not people care about it, know about it, or even if it's not useful for a player. It makes perfect sense to tell Gyges or the slave owner, "According to morality, you ought to free your slaves," but Gyges can also reply, "I don't care" without any contradiction. Luckily, most people are not in a position to exploit others without any consequences, and morality is almost always a better way of maximizing long-term interests than force. The philosopher Philippa Foot (1972) once called this a "system of hypothetical imperatives." The point is that morality doesn't have magical powers to make people change their behavior, but it still correctly describes a set of better and worse behaviors for self-interested agents in most circumstances. With an understanding of the *function* of human moral judgments, we can now use this to understand the purpose of moral theories and evaluate which ones are best.

Chapter summary

- The evolutionary hypothesis, originally advocated by Darwin, posits that moral judgments are the product of evolutionary pressures for cooperative behavior in otherwise self-interested organisms.

- A "cooperation problem" can be formally defined as any interaction between self-interested agents, where both players acting in rational self-interest will lead to results which have universal (Pareto) improvements for each player.
- Examples of cooperation problems include the Prisoner's Dilemma and Stag Hunt.
- Hundreds of algorithms have been developed for playing cooperation games like Prisoner's Dilemma, but the most successful ones all share essential features with a strategy called Tit-for-Tat, which cooperates with cooperators and defects with defectors.
- There is a structural resemblance between rules in our intuitive moral grammar like the Intentional Harm Rule and the Retribution Rule and the rules of Tit-for-Tat. This can be used as an "optimality modeling" argument that our moral grammar has an adaptive function of producing cooperative behavior.
- The position that "morality is cooperation" involves the meta-ethical commitments to realism, naturalism, instrumentalism about values, and acknowledging the possibility of amoralism.
- Any top-down or bottom-up approaches to modeling cooperative robots will wind up producing results very much like our intuitive moral grammar, and this carries with it the same limitations of undecidability in moral dilemma situations.

Notes

1 For simplicity, most of the games here will be simultaneous, complete-knowledge games without signaling, and the payoffs will be represented with ordinal preferences rather than cardinal utilities.
2 Formally, if we have a game with n players, where A_i are the available actions for player i, $A = A1 \times A2 \times, ...An$ are the action profiles for each player, and $f_1(x) ... f_n(x)$ are the utility functions for the players in each outcome, $x \in A$, then an outcome will be a Nash Equilibrium (NE) whenever: $\forall (i,x) \in A : f_i(NE_i, NE_{-i}) \geq f_i(x_i, NE_{-i})$
3 Using the same variables from the previous footnote, we can define a Pareto-optimal (PO) point as: $\forall (i,x) \in A, [f_a(x_a) > f_a(PO_a)] \rightarrow [f_b(x_b) < f_b(PO_b)]$
4 One might think that simply adding some finite number of iterations to the repeated Prisoner's Dilemma would immediately result in both players cooperating. After all, the two would eventually discover that it is in their best interest over the long run to always cooperate. However, the solution is not so simple. If the two players know that they are playing the game some finite number of times (say, 47 times), then on the last iteration (the 47th time), both players should defect, since the last iteration is effectively the same as a one-time Prisoner's Dilemma game. Yet if each player is surely going to defect on the 47th iteration, then the 46th iteration also becomes a one-time Prisoner's Dilemma game. The same holds for the 45th, and the 44th, until we work backwards and find that the rational strategy in any finite number of repeated Prisoner's Dilemma games is to always defect. As long as you know the last iteration T(n), defect will always be dominant, and this will make defecting dominant on T(n−1), and so on. This problem with the finitely repeated Prisoner's Dilemma game could be eliminated if we were to prevent both players from knowing when the last iteration of the game would be. This could be theoretically done by making the repetitions infinite. There have been solutions developed for the infinitely repeated Prisoner's Dilemma game, but they face a difficult problem to

overcome: infinite games result in infinite payoffs for each outcome, as long as there is some chance of not getting a 0 on every iteration. Though the problem can be overcome with a clever method involving the discounting of future payoffs in relation to present payoffs, the fact still remains that infinitely repeated games are not a model of real social interactions. A better model would be to examine an indefinite but finite sequence of Prisoner's Dilemma games between two players, where the conclusion of iterations is determined by a random event not knowable to either party. This appears to be a more realistic model, since social interactions are often repeated, but neither party is usually aware of exactly how many times.

5 It is also misleading to describe TFT as a single strategy. More accurately, it's a family of strategies, just like GRIM. What each of the TFT variations has in common is that they are all nice, not envious, punishing, and forgiving. Yet some versions might be more nice, or more forgiving, than others. Some of these variations might even do a better job of addressing the shortcomings of Rappaport's original algorithm. Consider the following strategy:

> TIT-FOR-TWO TATS: Cooperate on the first move. If the other player cooperates, continue playing Dove. If the other player defects twice in a row, switch to Hawk.

This strategy still has the advantages of still being nice, punishing, and forgiving, but it is less quick to punish and forgive than the original strategy.

6 Philosophers like Sharon Street (1996) and Richard Joyce (2006) have argued for many years that evolutionary biology has negative implications for moral realism. Street defines moral realism as the claim that "facts about natural-normative identities ... are independent of our evaluative attitudes." In one sense, it is clear what Street has in mind here: the distinction between something like a social convention which is true because humans agree on it, and what John Searle calls a "brute fact," like how many electrons are in an atom of gold. But in another sense, it's vague exactly what we mean by being "independent" of evaluative attitudes. While strategies in cooperation games are clearly about human interactions, they're also different from social conventions. Instead, they're abstract objects. Even if nobody believed that TFT is a superior strategy in cooperation games, it would still be true, so this is not dependent on anybody's evaluations, unlike the belief that Donald Trump is currently the president. Yet the existence of strategies is dependent on human interactions. This is not much different from a claim like "sleep improves memory;" which obviously depends in some way on the existence of people who sleep and have memory. Importantly though, it doesn't depend on their *evaluating* the statement to be true. A better formulation of the realist position is that the statement is not made true by people's attitudes *about that statement*. In this sense, the evolutionary story presented here presents no challenge to realism about moral truths. These truths just turn out to be a set of abstract objects describing human interactions.

7 In some views of what a representation is, this view implies that moral judgments *represent* the class of strategies like TFT. If that's true, we would be very interested in metaphysical questions about strategies, since this might make the difference in whether we can say that morality "really exists" or not, i.e., the question of moral realism. Many authors seem to think that, if moral claims refer to a set of strategies for reproductive success, then morality does not actually exist.

References

Axelrod, Robert (1984). *The Evolution of Cooperation*. New York: Basic Books.
Binmore, Ken (1994). *Playing Fair: Game Theory and the Social Contract I*. Cambridge, MA: MIT Press.

Danielson, Peter (1992). *Artificial Morality: Virtuous Robots for Virtual Games.* New York: Routledge.
Darwin, Charles (1845). *Journal of Researches into the Natural History and Geology of the Countries Visited during the Voyage of H.M.S. Beagle Round the World [Voyage of the Beagle].* New York: Harper and Brothers Publishers.
Darwin, Charles (1859). *On the Origin of Species by Means of Natural Selection,* facsimile reprint of 1st edition. Cambridge, MA: Harvard University Press.
Darwin, Charles (1871). *The Descent of Man and Selection in Relation to Sex,* facsimile reprint of 1st edition, Princeton, NJ: Princeton University Press.
Dawkins, Richard (1976). *The Selfish Gene.* Oxford: Oxford University Press.
Dawkins, Richard (1986). *The Blind Watchmaker: Why the Evidence for Evolution Reveals a Universe without Design.* New York: W. W. Norton.
Foot, Philippa (1972). "Morality as a System of Hypothetical Imperatives." *Philosophical Review,* 81, 305–316.
Gauthier, David (1986). *Morals by Agreement.* Oxford: Clarendon Press.
Hobbes, Thomas (1651). *Leviathan.* New York: Hackett.
Hume, David (1738). *A Treatise of Human Nature.* Oxford: Oxford University Press.
Joyce, Richard (2006). *The Evolution of Morality.* Cambridge, MA: MIT Press.
Jurisic, Marko & Kermek, Dragutin & Konecki, Mladen (2012). "A Review of Iterated Prisoner's Dilemma Strategies." MIPRO, 2012 Proceedings of the International Convention, 1093–1097.
Krebs, John & Erichsen, Jonathan & Webber, Michael, & Charnov, Eric (1977). "Optimal Prey Selection in the Great Tit (Parus Major)." *Animal Behavior,* 25, 30–38.
Nowak, Martin (2006). *Evolutionary Dynamics: Exploring the Equations of Life.* Cambridge, MA: Harvard University Press.
Rousseau, Jean-Jacques (1762). "The Social Contract." In: Victor Gourevitch (trans.) *The Social Contract and Other Later Political Writings* (1997). Cambridge: Cambridge University Press.
Searle, John (1995). *The Construction of Social Reality.* New York: Free Press.
Skyrms, Brian (1996). *Evolution of the Social Contract.* Cambridge: Cambridge University Press.
Street, Sharon (1996). "A Darwinian Dilemma for Realist Theories of Value." *Philosophical Studies,* 127, 109–166.

3
THEORIES

Every Saturday afternoon, your robot personal assistant buys you groceries and brings them back to your apartment. On one of these Saturday afternoons, you notice that the robot only brought back a third of the groceries on your list. You say, "Robot! What's the problem? Why didn't you buy all the groceries?" The robot sheepishly responds, "I did, but then I passed by two homeless men on the way here."

If we program a robot to recognize a rule like "don't violate property rights," and also a rule like "don't allow people to suffer if you can prevent it," there will sometimes be situations like the one above, where respecting property will allow people to suffer, and saving lives will violate property. This might sound like a silly problem, but it's one that most people in wealthy industrialized countries face almost every day. As the philosopher Peter Singer (1972) has pointed out, every time you spend money on luxuries like movies, sushi, or beer, that is money you could have been spending on people who are currently suffering and dying of easily preventable causes like malnourishment or malaria. Singer illustrates this problem with a famous thought-experiment:

> [I]f I am walking past a shallow pond and see a child drowning in it, I ought to wade in and pull the child out. This will mean getting my clothes muddy, but this is insignificant, while the death of the child would presumably be a very bad thing.
>
> *(Singer, 1972)*

If you agree that it would be morally wrong to allow a child to drown in a shallow pond to save your expensive clothes, then it appears inconsistent to allow children to die of malaria when you could be donating money to charities rather than buying expensive new clothes. And a robot programmed to save children from dying ponds would immediately start giving your money away as soon as it has any control over your bank account.

When I present Singer's drowning child scenario to students, they usually start out by trying to find some explanation for why buying luxuries is doing more overall good than giving to charity. Maybe there's no way of preventing those misfortunes, or the charities are all corrupt, or the entire economy will collapse if you don't buy new jeans. But these are all pretty implausible stories. The next step is that students will start generating reasons why saving a drowning child in the pond is different from saving a distant child. Our intuitive moral grammar uses mechanisms like empathy to identify who counts as a moral patient, so the suffering of people in front of you is more salient than the suffering of people in a distant country. However, most students quickly acknowledge that these mechanisms are arbitrary ways of deciding whose suffering is more or less valuable. The last step in the debate is when students make remarks like: "You own your money, so you can spend it however you like," or "You don't intend the deaths of those people, you just expect them." These are principles that allow a wealthy person to go on enjoying luxuries, but also imply that allowing the child to drown would be permissible, since you didn't intend the child to be there, and don't have any positive obligations towards her. This is the beginning of a moral theory.

Moral philosophers have spent centuries developing sophisticated theories like utilitarianism and libertarianism to go beyond our intuitive moral judgments in making predictions about which actions are wrong or permissible. In the sciences, a *theory* is a set of clearly defined terms organized into laws or principles that make objectively measurable predictions. Theories aim at both internal consistency and external predictive accuracy. By using theories, moral philosophers are employing a powerful tool. The demand for clarity and consistency pushes moral philosophers to articulate ways of measuring entities like "property" or "harm"; it also pushes them to create general rules that can resolve conflicts between violations of property and harm. Principles like "act in a way that maximizes happiness" will sacrifice property to prevent suffering, even at great distances. Other principles, like "don't intentionally violate rights" will allow suffering that is not initiated by the agent. Just like our moral grammar or strategies for cooperation games, theories like utilitarianism and libertarianism can be turned into algorithms. But if each theory is internally consistent and mutually incompatible, which *should* we program into our machines? I propose that a moral theory, just like a scientific one, must be more than just internally consistent. It must also make external predictions that can be used to evaluate the theory. This chapter argues that moral theories are *rationalizations*; attempts to clarify and generalize our adaptive moral grammar. This means that they can be evaluated by how effectively they solve cooperation problems.

Programming theories

In an *Intro to Ethics* class like the one I've taught for several years, students spend the first half of the class learning about different moral theories. Here are some of the most historically influential candidates:

Utilitarianism: Actions are wrong whenever their consequences produce more overall suffering for everyone, and permissible when their consequences result in more net happiness. Anyone whose happiness is affected by an action should be considered in evaluating that action. Consequences are usually measured in terms of probability, with more likely happiness counting for more than less likely happiness. Most harmful actions are usually wrong, but sometimes it may be acceptable to cause some suffering for generating greater overall happiness. Historical advocates include Jeremy Bentham and John Stuart Mill.

Natural rights libertarianism: Actions are wrong whenever they cross a rights boundary. Rights are natural protective entities that can be pictured as surrounding an individual, her actions, and her property. They are not to be confused with legal rights, which are given by a government. A right can only be removed with the consent of its bearer. Thus, it is morally wrong to cross the boundary of an individual, impede her actions, or damage her property, because it violates her rights. However, once a rights boundary is eliminated, any actions are permissible. Historical advocates include John Locke and Robert Nozick.

Kantian ethics: Actions are wrong because they can't be universally applied as a rule to all other people without producing logical inconsistency. For example, if the action of homicide were extended to everybody at once, it would also eliminate the actions of the person doing the killing. Although consent is important for Kant's moral theory, people can't rationally consent to actions that will undermine or demean their reason itself, so rational people can't sell themselves into slavery, commit suicide, or otherwise treat themselves like an animal. This also corresponds to the "categorical imperative," which commands respect for every rational agent as something with dignity rather than a tool or physical object. Actions are wrong because of inconsistency in the agent's mind, so agents must be acting intentionally for an action to be morally relevant. This produces the principle of double-effect: my action can have a good and a bad effect, but if I intend the good one and just foresee the bad one, then the action is permissible. Historical advocates include Immanuel Kant (probably the most famous Kantian) and Judith Thomson.

Virtue ethics: Wrong actions are the product of a human being who is not in the correct kind of state. There are certain states that enable humans to flourish, and these states are called virtuous states. If a human being is in the right kind of state, then she will necessarily do the right kind of action. Thus, if we want to know whether murder and cheating are morally wrong, we can ask whether a virtuous person who flourishes would perform these actions. This is not so much a matter of self-interest as it is being in a general healthy or well-rounded state for human beings. Virtue ethics is usually opposed to fixed rules, and accepts that sometimes a virtuous person will act like a utilitarian and other times she will act like a libertarian, as long as their character is strong. Historical advocates include Aristotle and Elizabeth Anscombe.

These theories all agree that homicide and battery are morally wrong, but they have different reasons for *why* these actions are wrong. Utilitarianism focuses on suffering to the victim, libertarianism focuses on the transgression of a rights-boundary without consent, and Kantian ethics focuses on the inconsistent or disrespectful intentions of the agent. These theories also have interesting disagreements in unusual cases, and handle dilemmas like the drowning child scenario very differently.

There have been several efforts to design algorithms based on each of these theories. Let's first consider a utilitarian algorithm developed by Michael Anderson, Susan Anderson, and Chris Armen (2005). The utilitarian algorithm uses self-report measurements of the intensity of pleasure or pain, the duration of pleasure or pain, and the likelihood of the event:

> [The utilitarian algorithm] presents the user with an input screen that prompts for the name of an action and the name of a person affected by that action as well as a rough estimate of the amount (very pleasurable, somewhat pleasurable, not pleasurable or displeasurable, somewhat displeasurable, very displeasurable) and likelihood (very likely, somewhat likely, not very likely) of pleasure or displeasure that the person would experience if this action were chosen. The user continues to enter this data for each person affected by the action and this input is completed for each action under consideration.

The calculation over this data takes the product of each of these input values (the intensity, duration, and likelihood), then sums those products for every agent, and outputs the action with the highest sum. For example, imagine we have two options: (A1) save the drowning child or (A2) keep our nice new shoes dry. If my shoes get wet, I will probably receive a mildly displeasurable payoff, say a loss of 200 points (roughly translated as U.S. dollar units of suffering), and some frustration over losing the shoes that will last for a few days. In civil court, these costs are called "pain and suffering," and let's say this will be 20 units of suffering for a few days. However, if the child dies, this will prevent many years of her enjoying an otherwise happy life, and also cause immense suffering for her friends and family that will last for years. Putting a number value on the suffering of losing a child might seem cruel, but it's the kind of thing that governments and insurance companies must do regularly. For example, the U.S. government currently pays families of soldiers killed in action a $500,000 death benefit, and most insurance companies (following Medicare) use a standard of $50,000 per life year to determine whether dialysis will be covered for terminal patients. Let's assume the child is 9 years old and will live an average life span, which is 81 years for females in the U.S. in 2017. Using these numbers as a back-of-the-envelope estimate, we might add the −500,000 points to the −50,000 points over the remaining 72 years of the child's life, to give a total loss of −4,100,000 units. Armed with these assumptions, we can estimate that saving the child's life will result in −260 utility points for me, and no gains or losses for the child or her family. Allowing the child to die will result in no gains or losses for me, but −4,100,000 utility points for the child and her family. Even if we adjust the likelihoods to make it a 1 percent chance that the child will die in the pond without my help, the value of saving the child still outweighs the value of keeping my nice shoes. To be precise, the probability of the child surviving would need to be greater than 99.994 percent for me to prefer keeping my new shoes dry. Incidentally, this is why utilitarians often say that we have a moral obligation to give luxury wealth to charity, even if there is only a 1 percent chance of saving someone's life.

Compare this result to a Kantian algorithm developed by Thomas Powers (2006), where a machine rejects actions whenever they are the result of a contradiction in its background beliefs, purposes (intentions), and context. For instance, in the context of physician-assisted suicide, Kantians traditionally approve of "allowing people to die" on the grounds that the intentions and goals of removing life support are merely to prevent suffering rather than to end life (Steinbock, 2016). On the other hand, Kantians do not approve of administering lethal injections, even if this would prevent much more overall suffering, since there is a contradiction between the purpose of the action (helping a person) and the background beliefs about lethal injections (they destroy a person's self). This is the "principle of double effect," which Thomas Aquinas (1274) describes as a distinction between those effects of an action which are intended and those which are merely expected. On these grounds, Aquinas argues that killing people in self-defense is permissible:

> Nothing hinders one act from having two effects, only one of which is intended, while the other is beside the intention. … Accordingly, the act of self-defense may have two effects: one, the saving of one's life; the other, the slaying of the aggressor.

If taken to the extreme, this principle holds that allowing others to die is always permissible, so long as the purpose of the action is not to kill. For instance, Judith Thomson (1971) describes a scenario where a famous actor (Henry Fonda) could easily cure a terminal patient's disease by simply touching them on the forehead, and she insists that he has no moral obligations to do so, even though the action would obviously be very nice. A Kantian algorithm like the one proposed by Powers may allow us to let the drowning child die, on the grounds that our purpose of performing these actions is to keep our nice new shoes, and there is nothing inconsistent about keeping new shoes.

I'm not aware of any researchers who have developed an algorithm based on natural rights libertarianism, but we could easily imagine the broad outlines of what it would look like. The most important components of this theory are the distinction between positive and negative obligations. A positive obligation is a duty that involves taking some action, like jumping into a pond or pulling a switch. On the other hand, a negative obligation is a duty that involves taking no action, like refraining from stealing, killing, or lying. Natural rights theorists are famous for claiming that there are no positive moral obligations. Thus, a libertarian algorithm would identify a category of actions that violates people's life, health, liberty, or property, and introduce hard constraints to never perform these actions without explicit consent. All other actions are categorized as permissible. In the case of the drowning child, the action of refraining from saving a person from drowning will always be permissible, since it involves *inaction*. In fact, forcing someone to sacrifice their property in order to save someone's life would always be morally wrong, since that would be crossing a rights boundary (a negative obligation) in the service of helping someone in need (a positive obligation).

Finally, some machine ethicists like Wallach and Allen (2008) have argued that we can use the connection between virtue ethics and machine learning techniques to avoid all the complications of the other moral theories. Rather than designing a method for evaluating pleasure intensity, or evaluating contradictions between intended goals and background beliefs, we can train a machine to produce responses based on negative and positive feedback from a large database of human responses to similar cases. For example, Bruce McLaren's (2003) algorithm called *Truth-Teller* uses a machine learning approach to engineering ethics problems. Using data from the judgments of ethics boards over a range of hundreds of cases, *Truth-Teller* extends features extracted from that set to novel cases (this kind of case-based reasoning is similar to how judges make decisions based on case histories, and doctors make judgments based on clinical examples).

How would a virtuous learning algorithm apply to the drowning child scenario? Since most humans in our society view distance as a morally relevant feature, this system might learn a trade-off function between how close the suffering is, how much suffering is perceived to be happening, and how much an agent must sacrifice to prevent that suffering. Such a function will inevitably be different based on different groups of people that are in the "training set." Most virtue ethics algorithms will probably abandon new shoes to save the drowning child, but not to save malnourished children in distant countries. Of course, this leaves the problem from the beginning of this chapter: when the robot passes by homeless people, will it give away your groceries? Perhaps another feature that this learning algorithm might extract from our actual judgments is an identification of what situations constitute "emergencies," and which do not. As behavioral economists have discovered, emergencies have an emotional salience that more permanent or long-term problems do not, even though this emotional salience often prevents people from making more rational decisions like saving for retirement or taking action against global warming.

We face the problem once again: which of these moral theories *should* we program into a machine? This all depends on exactly what the purpose of a moral theory is, and where specifically moral values come from.

Instrumental values

By the end of *Intro to Ethics*, students are sometimes left skeptical about the whole business of moral theorizing. After the first clash between a utilitarian and a libertarian, they quickly realize that there's no common ground to measure which theory is correct. In the natural sciences, when two theories come to different conclusions, both sides will try to produce some objective measurement that will resolve the disagreement to everyone's satisfaction. But what observations do we use to test moral theories against each other? As philosopher Gilbert Harman (1977) once pointed out, it's not as if people who have moral disagreements are observing different things. It seems like both sides have access to all the same empirical facts.

It's not only students and philosophers who have come to this conclusion: many researchers in machine ethics have come to these skeptical conclusions about a single moral theory. In their book, *Moral Machines: Teaching Robots Right from Wrong* (2008), Wendell Wallach and Colin Allen express the kind of attitude that most college students have at the end of an introductory ethics class: given all the different normative theories, it seems arbitrary to pick one of these as the single theory to program into machines as opposed to others. They write:

> Given the range of perspectives regarding the morality of specific values, behaviors, and lifestyles, perhaps there is no single answer to the question of whose morality or what morality should be implemented in AI. Just as people have different moral standards, there is no reason why all computational systems must conform to the same code of behavior.

If this is true, then what could we possibly use to settle these disagreements and evaluate which theory is best? Do we just pick a team, like in sports, based on which colors are our favorite? Most philosophy teachers do allow their students to pick whichever theory appeals to them the most, but only insist that the students are consistent in accepting all of its predictions. If you're a utilitarian, you've got to admit that it's sometimes acceptable to harm a few people to help the majority. If you're a libertarian, you've got to admit that consensual cannibalism and death-sports are acceptable. If you're a Kantian, you've got to admit that lying is always wrong, even to save the entire world. When someone is willing to accept all the weirdness that comes along with a theory ("biting the bullet"), the debate usually comes to an unresolved conclusion.

Internal consistency is necessary for any good theory, but it can't be *all* we use to evaluate the theory. There is an infinite number of internally consistent but completely ridiculous moral theories. Here's one that no one takes seriously: "tacotilitarianism." It says that actions are right whenever they increase the total number of tacos in the universe, and wrong when they decrease the total number of tacos. There's nothing inconsistent about that theory, but it's completely crazy. The theories that people take seriously (utilitarianism, libertarianism, Kantian ethics) aren't just internally consistent; they also match most of our pretheoretical intuitions about which actions are wrong and right. This might be necessary, but even *this* isn't sufficient to narrow down a single unique theory. Instead, like scientific theories, there needs to be some outside measurement used to confirm or falsify a theory's predictions.

What could an external measurement possibly look like for a moral theory? The heart of this problem is what's known as the distinction between *facts* and *values*. Scientific theories are descriptive, which means they're about what the world is like. On the other hand, moral theories are about what the world *ought* to be like. The methods for discovering what *is* true or false can't be used to evaluate and falsify what *ought* to be true or false. If we concede right away that facts are irrelevant to evaluating moral theories, then we've already lost any way to evaluate them, aside from being internally consistent and matching our intuitive judgments. Sure, values could exist in a mysterious realm outside our world of facts, but this raises a wet laundry bag of ancient problems that we won't even try to deal with here. So where do values come from?

The key to understanding values is realizing that talk about objectively better and worse states also exists in engineering and medicine. Structural engineers have no problem saying that a suspension bridge made of glass is a bad idea, and an objectively worse way to build it than using steel. Physicians also have no problem saying that smoking is bad for health, or that drinking water daily is good for health, and that these claims are objectively true. This is because engineering and medicine are directed towards specific goals like health and building sound structures. In other words, they provide *reasons for action*, rather than reasons for belief. It's true that antibiotics are a better treatment for an infection than rubbing a potato on it, but this is only true *relative to the goal* of healing the patient. Once we make this goal explicit, the claim looks like this: "If you want to heal the patient's infection, antibiotics are the best available way of doing it." Assuming that everyone wants to be healthy (a fair assumption), it makes sense to leave the goal implicit and say: "The patient ought to take antibiotics!" These kinds of values are called *instrumental* values. Since this is the only way I've ever seen to make sense of values without the aid of magic, I suggest that we think of values in ethics the same way.

This idea was rejected by Immanuel Kant (1785), who insisted that moral reasons are not aimed at any goal at all. According to Kant, moral reasons for action are different from instrumental ones. For example, the claim "You ought to take care of your children," is fundamentally different from instrumental claims like "If you want to avoid going to jail, you ought to take care of your children." Kant insists that the second claim, which he called a *hypothetical* command, is not a moral one at all, and anyone who thinks it is just misses the point of ethics. Hypothetical claims are common in engineering ("If you want to build a bridge that stays up, you should use steel") and medicine ("If you want to be healthy, you should stop smoking"), but not in morality. Moral commands are what he calls *categorical*, meaning that they don't depend on any particular goals or desires. It's a mistake to say: "If you want to do *x*, then you ought to take care of your kids." Instead, a moral claim is: "You ought to take care of your kids, period!" And yes, I am aware that I just ended a sentence with both the word *period* and an exclamation mark.

The problem with categorical reasons is that they're completely incomprehensible. I literally don't understand what it would mean to tell someone: "You must study for the test, no matter what you want or care about." In fact, it seems to contradict what it means for something to be a reason for action. As Hume (1739) pointed out, reasons for action are *practically guiding*, meaning they provide some motivation for the person endorsing them. Beliefs like "Andromeda is the closest galaxy to the Milky Way" are never themselves enough to motivate someone to care about the Andromeda galaxy. I could easily believe that Andromeda is the closest galaxy and not care about it at all. However, moral beliefs like "You ought to take care of your children" *are* practically guiding, since it's impossible to genuinely believe that you ought to take care of your children and at the same time not care about them. Moral claims can't simultaneously be categorical and practically guiding. Since they're obviously practically guiding, we must abandon the idea of categorical commands.

Was Kant completely mistaken that moral claims are categorical? In part, yes. But there are plenty of ways that a categorical command can be rhetorically useful. Imagine a rug salesman who is negotiating with some stubborn customer. The salesman says: "I don't even want to sell this rug, it's too nice, I shouldn't have put it out on the sales floor. I'm going to take it back to the stockroom." This is obviously false and we all know it. Why is he even talking about the rug if he doesn't want to sell it? But acting like he doesn't care is a clever negotiating tactic. Similarly, pretending that a student must study for his exam *no matter what he cares about* is an especially strong negotiating stance to get him to study. In his book, *Confusion of Tongues* (2014), Stephen Finlay has convincingly argued that categorical commands like "Don't steal!" are cleverly disguised hypothetical commands like "If you want this goal, don't steal," where the goal is projected onto agents (or even onto the fabric of reality).

If moral theories are about instrumental values, then we need to identify what goals they're trying to accomplish. Not surprisingly, I think the goal of moral theories is the same as the function of our evolved moral intuitions: producing cooperative behavior among self-interested organisms. Theories like Kantian ethics and libertarianism appear to be about real entities like *rights* and *dignity* but these entities don't really exist. Instead, they are rationalizations created to clarify and generalize our moral grammar and maximize individual interests in repeated cooperation games.

Rationalizations

Friedrich Nietzsche (1886) suggested that moral principles are nothing more than "the personal confession of its author and a kind of involuntary and unconscious memoir." More recently, the psychologist Jonathan Haidt (2001) has argued that Nietzsche was correct; most reasons that people give for their moral beliefs are rationalizations to justify their own intuitions. Haidt's argument for this is based on *moral dumbfounding*, where people are presented with intuitively disgusting scenarios like the following, and are then asked to justify why the actions are wrong:

> Julie and Mark are brother and sister. They are traveling together in France on summer vacation from college. One night they are staying alone in a

cabin near the beach. They decide that it would be interesting and fun if they tried making love. At the very least it would be a new experience for each of them. Julie was already taking birth control pills, but Mark uses a condom too, just to be safe. They both enjoy making love, but they decide not to do it again. They keep that night as a special secret, which makes them feel even closer to each other. What do you think about that? Was it OK for them to make love?

According to Haidt, people presented with this scenario give obviously pathetic reasons for why this action was wrong, like "their children would have higher likelihood of abnormalities" or "they might encourage others to do this." These reasons are quickly shot down by the experimenters reminding them that the story rules out those possibilities. Eventually, after a long string of reasons are easily dismissed, the participants in Haidt's experiment simply dig in and insist that the affair was *just wrong*, even if they can't explain why. That last part is crucial to the dumbfounding process; when someone is desperately looking for some reason in the absence of any good candidates, it suggests those reasons are not the real cause of their beliefs and actions. Haidt concludes that normative theories are not what cause moral judgments, but the other way around: they are the "rational tail" that is wagged by an "emotional dog" (although he would probably now rephrase this as the "intuitive dog").

What's bad about rationalization? Take the following example: a wife is cheating on her husband, and she defends it by saying: "He'd do the same to me, if he had the chance!" This might be true. But if her story is a rationalization, it's not because it's false or offered after the fact, but because it's not the *real* reason for her actions. As I've suggested in a paper with Jonathan Hricko (2017), rationalizations are bad because they're somehow *disconnected* from the action or belief you're justifying. In the cheating wife case, the fact that her husband would do the same has no impact on whether she cheats or not.

One of the best ways to identify a rationalization is with the dumbfounding procedure used by Haidt. Dumbfounding involves asking someone whether they would hypothetically still believe or act the same way, were that reason defeated. When the cheating wife insists: "My husband would do the same to me," we might ask her, "Well, what if he didn't? Would you still be cheating on him?" If this is a rationalization, the answer will almost certainly be "Yes … because …" followed by a search for other explanations. It's astounding how effective this method can be. Dumbfounding works because a rationalization is causally unrelated to people's actual beliefs and actions, so defeating them will not change anything. Another feature of rationalizations is how quick people are to immediately discard them and then move on to another reason. For example, the cheating wife might continue: "… I would still cheat, because he never showed me enough appreciation." Once again, this might be true, but we can do some more dumbfounding by asking "What if he *did* show you more appreciation?" If she gives yet another reason, this is more evidence that these were just rationalizations.

As someone who has taught ethics courses at every level, I can testify to the massive amounts of dumbfounding I've observed in the classroom. The best example is vegetarianism, since most students are very committed to eating meat, but there aren't very many good moral reasons for doing it. My opening question in this debate is simple: "Give me one good reason why it is acceptable to eat an animal, but not a human." All of them try; in fact, this discussion is the most rowdy and exciting debate of the year. I've played the vegetarianism game for several years, and the first thing you realize after playing it many times is that all the reasons that students provide are predictable and terrible. By terrible, I don't just mean weak. I mean painfully, confusingly, exasperatingly *terrible*. In a recent interview on Sam Harris's podcast, *Waking Up*, the psychologist Paul Bloom remarks on this:

> I've heard defenses of meat eating, and they're some of the worst arguments I've ever heard in my life ... arguments that wouldn't be taken seriously in any other domain.

I've found it's almost hilarious how easy it is to defeat these reasons. Students *laugh out loud* when they realize this. Even the student who presents the argument will immediately concede, usually with a murmur of "Oh, right." To illustrate the vegetarianism game, imagine it as a Socratic dialogue, where Socrates just asks questions that generalize the principle to other cases, showing that these are reasons the *student herself* would never accept in other contexts:

Socrates: Give me one good reason why it's acceptable to eat an animal, but not a human.
Student: We need protein to survive.
Socrates: It's impossible to be a healthy vegetarian in a wealthy industrialized society?
Student: Oh, right. Well ... Animals eat other animals.
Socrates: Animals also rape other animals, is that acceptable for humans to do?
Student: Oh, right. Well ... It's natural and traditional for humans to eat other animals.
Socrates: Slavery and rape might be natural and traditional, does that make them acceptable?
Student: Oh, right. Well ... Animals don't care about being eaten.
Socrates: Animals in factory farming conditions wouldn't prefer to be free?
Student: Oh, right. Well ... It's wrong to eat members of your own species.
Socrates: It's permissible for Captain Kirk to eat Mr. Spock?
Student: Oh, right. Well ... Animals don't have language and higher cognitive abilities.
Socrates: Babies and severely mentally disabled people don't have language and higher cognitive abilities; can we eat them?
Student: Oh, right. Well ... Animals don't have any rights.

Socrates: It's permissible to rape and torture animals for no purpose?
Student: Oh, right. Well ... God says it's permissible to eat animals.
Socrates: If God said it is permissible to eat humans, it would be?
Student: Oh, right. Well ... Eating humans is unhealthy.
Socrates: If eating humans were healthy, it would be permissible?
Student: Oh, right. Well ... It's permissible to kill animals for population control.
Socrates: It's permissible to kill humans for population control?
Student: Oh, right. Well ... Circle of life.
Socrates: What does that even mean?
Student: I don't know.

If this game is too easy, try a more difficult game where the challenge is to explain why eating cows and sheep is acceptable, but eating cats and monkeys isn't. These games are difficult because the student is trying to come up with a rule that generalizes to humans and animals while preserving all our moral intuitions. The problem is that this is impossible; our evolved moral grammar uses many different processes for identifying moral patients (genetic relatedness, similarity to humans, familiarity, empathy), and most of them produce inconsistent results. We might use genetic relatedness to prefer humans to animals, but empathy prevents us from torturing or raping animals. Monkeys are similar to humans and cats are familiar, even though neither of these is related. People are reaching desperately for some consistent theory that preserves all of these judgments, but such a solution is impossible. Just like in Haidt's experiments, the game never ends with students admitting that eating animals is wrong. Instead, they dig in and insist that eating animals "just is" acceptable, even if they can't explain why.

In addition to dumbfounding, the other important sign of rationalization is the existence of a better alternative explanation for the rationalizer's beliefs or actions. For example, the cheating wife *thinks* her actions are caused by the husband's lack of concern, but an alternative explanation for her actions is a desire for new partners. Joshua Greene has argued that moral theories based on rights are better explained as rationalizations of our moral psychology than by reference to actual objects in the world called "rights." This is also part of Haidt's argument: in the "Julie and Mark" scenario, people's opposition to harmless incest is better tracked by disgust responses than by concern about negative social consequences or genetic abnormalities. In the vegetarianism debate, the student's defense of meat-eating is better tracked by in-group preferences than the absurd reasons provided. In his astoundingly titled article, *The Secret Joke of Kant's Soul* (2008), Greene illustrates this idea with a story:

> Your friend Alice goes on many dates, and after each one she reports back to you. When she extols the people she likes and complains about the ones she dislikes, she cites a great many factors. This one is brilliant. That one is self-absorbed.

This one has a great sense of humor. That one is a dud. And so on. But then you notice something: All the people she likes are exceptionally tall. Closer inspection reveals that after scores of dates over several years, she has not given the thumbs up to anyone who is less than six-foot-four, and has not turned down anyone over this height. (You plug Alice's dating data into your statistics software and confirm that height is a near perfect predictor of Alice's preferences.) Suddenly it seems that Alice's judgment is not what you had believed, and certainly not what she believes. Alice, of course, believes that her romantic judgments are based on a variety of complicated factors. But, if the numbers are to be believed, she basically has a height fetish, and all of her talk about wit and charm and kindness is mere rationalization.

Just like with Alice, if we can identify some factor that better explains people's moral judgments than the reasons they give, then the reasons are probably rationalizations. In an article with the more self-explanatory title: "Disgust Sensitivity Predicts Intuitive Disapproval of Gays" (2009), psychologist Yoel Inbar and colleagues found that ... you guessed it ... people's disgust sensitivity predicted their intuitive disapproval of gays. If most of these participants were asked why they disapproved of homosexuality, they might cite reasons like: "God disapproves of it in the Bible," "It's not natural," or "It leads to social problems." However, the correlation between their judgments and disgust responses provides a better alternative explanation.

I'm arguing that moral theories are rationalizations, fictions created to justify the outputs of our evolved moral grammar. This might sound bad for ethics, but not to worry. The good news about rationalizations is that they're movement in the *right direction*: developing consistent principles that extend our moral grammar into situations where harm is vague (like prostitution) or requires trade-offs between players (like the trolley problem). Once we recognize the purpose of moral theories, just like in engineering and medicine, it's possible to search for an outside way of evaluating moral theories beyond internal consistency.

Switching into manual mode

I'll borrow one more of Greene's (2014) analogies. Many cameras have both automatic and manual settings. Our automatic settings for moral judgments involve quick responses produced by an evolved moral grammar, and rationalizations which are built up around them to create consistency. As Greene notes, automatic settings on a camera work well for most normal situations, and there's usually no need to go through all the hard work of thinking about what you're trying to do with the camera: just "point and shoot." However, if you're trying to set up a difficult photograph, it might become necessary to learn a little about how a camera works and the best way to adjust the settings to create a well-focused image. Similarly, in most ordinary situations, our evolved moral grammar and strategies like Tit-for-Tat are sufficient to get by. However, in situations of vague harms and moral dilemmas, we need to "switch into manual mode" by understanding what our moral grammar is trying to do and moving beyond it.

Rationalizers are unable to test their moral principles, because they are unable to admit the instrumental goals driving their decisions. Once we discover that normative theories are developed to provide better and more consistent explanations for intuitive moral judgments, they can be evaluated by how effectively they solve the practical problem that moral grammar developed to solve. In addition to internal consistency, a moral theory should be evaluated by how effectively it produces universal Pareto-improvements on Nash Equilibria outcomes.

When we evaluate a principle like the utilitarian maxim: "Actions are morally wrong whenever they create more overall suffering than happiness," we need to ask: is this principle going to enforce cooperative behavior effectively? In the standard model for cooperation games, the Prisoner's Dilemma, it does. The utilitarian decision-procedure is: for each action, take the sum of payoffs for each player, and the action with the highest sum wins. In Prisoner's Dilemma, the sums for each outcome are: 3, 3, 2, 4 (Figure 3.1). The highest of these sums is 4, which corresponds to mutual cooperation, so that is the output of the utilitarian calculation.

Utilitarianism is a strong moral theory precisely because it provides a clear and objective way of measuring harm, while also extending to dilemma scenarios. In a classic dilemma situation, modeled by the trolley problem, the sum of payoffs in A1 (pull switch / push man) is always less than the sum of payoffs for A2 (do nothing), so A1 is always the right choice, regardless of whether it is produced by pulling a switch or pushing a man off the bridge (Figure 3.2).

Even if these results are sometimes counterintuitive, an internally consistent theory that produces cooperative behavior in all situations is by definition a successful moral theory. This is similar to scientific theories that are internally consistent and make observable predictions that are confirmed or falsified; just because they're surprising doesn't make them false.

PD Sums

Sean

	C	D
C	2, 2 (sum = 4)	3, 0 (sum = 3)
D	0, 3 (sum = 3)	1, 1 (sum = 2)

Ethan

FIGURE 3.1 Sums of payoffs in Prisoner's Dilemma outcomes, where C, C produces the highest value.

Trolley Problem Sums

States	P1	P2	P3	P4	P5	P6	Sums
Do Nothing	0	−99	−99	−99	−99	−99	= −495
Pull Switch	−99	0	0	0	0	0	= **−99**

FIGURE 3.2 Sums of payoffs in Trolley Problem outcomes.

Repugnant Prisoner's Dilemma

Sean

	C	D
C (Ethan)	2, 2	0, 1000
D (Ethan)	3, 0	1, 1

FIGURE 3.3 Payoffs in a Repugnant Prisoner's Dilemma, where one player stands to gain a much higher amount from exploitation than the other player.

There are, however, some cases where utilitarianism *fails* to produce cooperative behavior. Consider a game where we alter the payoffs in Prisoner's Dilemma such that one player receives *massive* payoffs from exploiting the other one.[1] In this game, the Nash Equilibrium point is still mutual defection, with a single universal Pareto-improvement of mutual cooperation. Let's call this the *Repugnant Prisoner's Dilemma* (Figure 3.3).

Classic utilitarianism says that the outcome of Sean exploiting Ethan in this game is so massively beneficial, that Ethan should just willingly agree to be exploited. But this fails the basic test of a moral theory: always producing cooperative behavior (defined as a universal Pareto-improvement from Nash Equilibria). A version of this objection was raised by the philosopher Derek Parfit (1984), called the *repugnant conclusion*. One of Parfit's repugnant conclusions he derives from utilitarianism is that a form of slavery might be justified if it makes the quality of life far greater for the masters than the slaves. But, as discussed in the previous chapter, if a moral theory allows for exploitation in *any* situations, it doesn't accomplish the evolutionary and contemporary function of morality.

Let's now consider a principle like libertarianism: "Actions are wrong whenever they cross an individual's rights-boundary without her consent." Advocates of this principle like Robert Nozick (1974) identify a rights violation as a causal relationship between the action of the agent and the loss of a patient's life, health, liberty, or property. In a typical interpretation of the Prisoner's Dilemma, the gains of one player are caused by the losses of another, so this is correctly interpreted as a rights violation. Exploitation would be wrong for either player, leading to mutual cooperation.

Libertarianism provides a clear standard for what counts as a rights violation, and it resolves dilemmas by not including any positive obligations. This means that every moral dilemma has a solution: do nothing. While the distinction between actions and omissions is useful, it fails to produce cooperative behavior in games like Stag Hunt (Figure 2.3). In this game, if I defect, the gains that I get (a hare dinner) are the same whether you defect or not. According to Nozick's theory of exploitation, this is like me having the same amount of money whether you are rich or poor, and suggests that no rights violation has occurred. Therefore, libertarianism does not provide any reason to cooperate in the SH game, which is one of the criteria for a moral theory. In contrast, utilitarianism *does* produce cooperation in SH, to the mutual benefit of all parties.

Hopefully this demonstrates how we can evaluate moral theories by "switching into manual mode" and testing whether they produce cooperative behavior in games where there exist mutual Pareto-improvements on the standard self-interested strategies. Importantly, it doesn't matter whether the entities in the theory (like *rights*) really exist. All that matters is that the theory is successful in solving cooperation problems.

To those familiar with the range of moral theories, this is also why I'm omitting any discussion of theories (or perhaps *anti-theories*) like virtue ethics and particularism: they lack clear categories and definitive predictions. Ideally, we want a consistent set of principles with an objective definition of harm that will not only match our evolved moral grammar in normal cooperation problems but also extend to dilemma situations. When it comes to producing cooperative results, utilitarianism succeeds in standard Prisoner's Dilemma and Stag Hunt, but fails in the Repugnant Prisoner's Dilemma. Libertarianism succeeds in both the standard and repugnant Prisoner's Dilemma, but fails in Stag Hunt. The next chapter will present a theory that satisfies all these criteria, while successfully extending to dilemma situations.

Chapter summary

- Efforts have recently been made to turn moral theories like utilitarianism, libertarianism, Kantian ethics, and virtue ethics into algorithms.
- Given that these theories are incompatible, we need a way of evaluating which one is best. Theories can be evaluated both *internally* and *externally*.
- Internal evaluation of a moral theory, just like a scientific theory, is based on the extent to which it contains objectively measurable categories, internally consistent rules, and unique predictions across a wide range of cases. Internal success is necessary for a moral theory, but not sufficient.
- External evaluation of a theory depends on the instrumental goals that moral theories are attempting to accomplish. Using dumbfounding arguments, there is good evidence that moral theories are *rationalizations*, or unconscious

attempts to clarify and generalize our intuitive moral grammar. This suggests that their instrumental goal is solving cooperation problems and generalizing to other noncooperative interactions (moral dilemmas).
- Utilitarianism is successful at this instrumental goal in most cases, but fails to produce cooperative behavior in "repugnant" versions of Prisoner's Dilemma. Libertarianism is also successful in most cases, but fails to produce cooperative behavior in Stag Hunt. The next chapter will describe a theory that succeeds in all cases.

Note

1 This requires the subtle but potentially objectionable move of switching over from ordinal to cardinal payoffs.

References

Anderson, Michael & Anderson, Susan, & Armen, Chris (2005). "Towards Machine Ethics." *AAAI-04 Workshop on Agent Orientations: Theory and Practice.*
Aquinas, Thomas (1274). *Summa Theologica*. Claremont, CA: Coyote Canyon Press. Reprinted in 2010.
Finlay, Stephen (2014). *Confusion of Tongues: A Theory of Normative Language*. Oxford: Oxford University Press.
Greene, Joshua (2008). "The Secret Joke of Kant's Soul." In: Walter Sinnott-Armstrong (ed.) *Moral Psychology, Vol. 2*. Cambridge, MA: MIT Press.
Greene, Joshua (2014). "Beyond Point-and-Shoot Morality: Why Cognitive (Neuro) Science Matters for Ethics." *Ethics*, 124, 695–726.
Haidt, Jonathan (2001). "The Emotional Dog and its Rational Tail." *Psychological Review*, 104, 814–834.
Harman, Gilbert (1977). *The Nature of Morality: An Introduction to Ethics*. Oxford: Oxford University Press.
Hricko, Jonathan & Leben, Derek (2017). "In Defense of Best-Explanation Debunking Arguments." *Review of Philosophy and Psychology*, 1–18.
Hume, David (1739). *A Treatise of Human Nature*. Oxford: Oxford University Press.
Inbar, Yoel & Pizarro, David & Knobe, Joshua & Bloom, Paul (2009). "Disgust Sensitivity Predicts Intuitive Disapproval of Gays." *Emotion*, 9, 435–443.
Kant, Immanuel (1785). *Groundwork on the Metaphysics of Morals*. Cambridge: Cambridge University Press.
Nietzsche, Friedrich (1886). *Beyond Good and Evil: Prelude to a Philosophy of the Future*. Trans. Walter Kaufman. New York: Vintage.
Nozick, Robert (1974). *Anarchy, State, and Utopia*. New York: Basic Books.
Parfit, Derek (1984). *Reasons and Persons*. Oxford: Clarendon Press.
Powers, Thomas (2006). "Prospects for a Kantian Machine." *IEEE Intelligent Systems 21.*
Singer, Peter (1972). *Famine, Affluence, and Morality*. New York: Oxford University Press.
Steinbock, Bonnie (2016). "The Intentional Termination of Life." Reprinted in Cahn, Steven M. (ed.) *Exploring Ethics*. New York: Oxford University Press.
Thomson, Judith (1971). "A Defense of Abortion." *Philosophy and Public Affairs*, 1, 47–66.
Wallach, Wendell & Allen, Colin (2008). *Moral Machines: Teaching Robots Right from Wrong*. New York: Oxford University Press.

4
CONTRACTARIANISM

The city of Königsberg was built in the former Prussia around a strategic island in the middle of the river Pregel, right where the river forks. In the eighteenth century, there were seven bridges around the middle of the city where this island sat: four connecting the island to the north and south sides, two connecting the peninsula to the north and south sides, and one connecting the island to the peninsula. The inhabitants of Königsberg had a game they would play on Sunday afternoons: try to visit each side of the river (the north side, south side, island, and peninsula), crossing each bridge only once. It was a difficult puzzle, and nobody had solved it. You can take a look at the map and try it yourself (Figure 4.1), it's actually more fun than it sounds.

In the 1730s, the mayor of nearby Danzig wrote a letter to perhaps the greatest mathematician of all time, Leonard Euler, presenting him with this problem. Euler's solution was elegant and simple, and as typical of Euler, wound up introducing several new areas of mathematics in the process. To solve the problem, Euler realized that the details of the bridges and their locations don't matter. How long the bridges are, what direction they're going, none of it matters. Instead, we can picture each land mass as an abstract node and each bridge as a line connecting the nodes (Figure 4.2).

In this abstract description, Euler saw that we want to visit every node, and enter on a different line than we leave (that is, exit a location from a different bridge than we entered), so the nodes will need an even number of lines connecting them. The exceptions to this are the starting and ending nodes, which can have an odd number of lines, since we don't need to enter or exit them. Because the locations in the city are connected by seven bridges, Euler discovered that the game was impossible to solve. This riddle, like many others, is dissolved by abstracting away from the details and asking what we want out of the problem in a very general sense.

60 Contractarianism

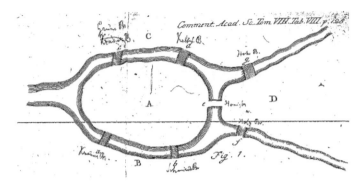

FIGURE 4.1 Leonard Euler's hand-drawn map of the seven bridges of Königsberg. Land masses are upper-case letters, and bridges are lower-case letters (courtesy: the Euler Online Archive).

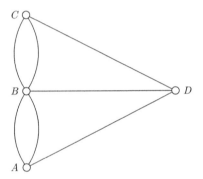

FIGURE 4.2 An abstract graph of the seven bridges of Königsberg, with the land masses denoted the same as Euler's drawing from Figure 4.1. The lower-case labels of bridges have been omitted.

I think of the Bridges of Königsberg when reading John Rawls's solution to the problem of cooperation. In trying to solve this problem, both our evolved moral grammar and various moral theories have come across *good enough* solutions through trial and error, a bit like how citizens of Königsberg tried to solve their puzzle by experimenting every Sunday. Coincidentally, Königsberg happens to be the hometown of Immanuel Kant, who would often take his regular walks across these bridges. But solutions to puzzles sometimes can't be obtained from experiments and trial and error, because these get muddled up in all the nonessential details of the problem. Instead, abstraction is the key. Stepping back from the details of the cooperation problem, the basic structure is that two people gain from mutual cooperation, but also risk being taken advantage of. Rawls realized that what is driving both parties to cheat is a divergence in interests. The more of their diverging interests you hide, the more cooperative behavior will result. Of course, you can't hide all of their interests, or else the motivation for cooperation over defection will disappear entirely. Thus, a *perfect* balance for accomplishing cooperation would hide all the differences that separate two players while leaving only the interests that they share. This is the idea of the *original position*, and the moral theory that follows from it.

In this chapter, I'll show how this insight of John Rawls, based on an abstract understanding of the problem of cooperation, produces the only procedure that necessarily ensures cooperative behavior in every situation. Thus, as I suggested in the previous chapter, it should be considered the best moral theory, and the approach we use in designing moral machines. In what follows, I'll outline the basic parts of this theory, called Contractarianism.

The original position

Thinking about the bare structure of a cooperation game, both players are self-interested, but to get to Pareto-optimality, they must also value the other person's interests. The closer the correlation between Player 1's interests and Player 2's interests, the more cooperation will occur. If we are trying to achieve *perfect* cooperation, we would need a perfect correlation: Player 1's interests are all identical to Player 2's interests. The most extreme way of doing this would be to literally think of the other player's interests as your own. This is the idea that's been rediscovered time and time again in world cultures and religions, "treat others as you treat yourself." But it seems to contradict the more fundamental assumption that players are self-interested. This is the challenge that Rawls is attempting to solve: treating another player's interests as equivalent to your own, while remaining self-interested.

As Rawls describes in *A Theory of Justice* (1971), his approach is to cover up knowledge about yourself in a *veil of ignorance*, which has the function of "[nullifying] the effects of specific contingencies which put men at odds and tempt them to exploit social and natural circumstances to their own advantage." In other words, covering up all the facts about one person's situation that makes it different from another person's situation. The veil of ignorance is designed to cover what Rawls calls the "subjective circumstances" that would otherwise prevent agents from cooperation, including their personal interests, life plans, and conceptions of the good. One way of thinking about this is that the subjective features covered by the veil are anything that distinguishes one person from someone else. This includes features like age, ethnicity, and weight, but also a person's religious and political beliefs, hobbies, career goals, and so on.

Not all information is covered by the veil of ignorance; a person still has access to all the features that human beings have in common, what Rawls calls "objective conditions," which is why they share the need for mutually advantageous cooperation in the first place. What are the facts about humans and their conditions that they all share? Think of features like: basic biological needs (sleep, food, water), and facts about human psychology, economics, and sociology. People would be aware that human beings often need incentives under the right conditions to work harder, that torture is not an effective method to gain information, and that people are healthier when they have access to clean drinking water.

When a person covers her subjective preferences under the veil of ignorance, leaving only objective features visible, she is in what Rawls calls the "original position." In the original position, you have access to information about the outcomes of every action, but you *don't* have access to knowledge about which person you wind up being in this distribution. Without access to information about your own place in a distribution of goods, from your perspective, *you could easily be anyone*. If I were going to sum up the big insight of the original position, it would be: *anonymity produces cooperation*. By anonymity, I mean the purest possible kind of anonymity, where even *you* don't know which person you are. Anybody in this state is motivated by pure self-interest to treat every person in a society equally.

The original position is often described as a thought-experiment, but this is a misnomer. It gives the impression that any principles following from it are somehow a matter of imagination, and nothing more than the result of conjuring an interesting scenario in what Dan Dennett cynically calls an *intuition-pump*. Rawls himself never uses the phrase "thought-experiment" to describe this idea in his original text, and I think the term is inaccurate. There is nothing experimental about the original position, nor is the goal to try to persuade people by manipulating their intuitions around an appealing story. Instead, it's an abstract description of a solution to the problem of cooperation, and a derivation of rules from this solution. That's why I introduce the theory by comparing it to Euler's Bridges of Königsberg solution. But it's true that the original position itself is a *pure fiction*, designed for the function of generating cooperative behavior, just like the entities in most other moral theories.

How are rules derived from the original position? Rawls claims that, within the original position, every self-interested player will be concerned to make the worst-off person in the group as best-off as she possibly can be. This is because, to put it bluntly, you could wind up being that person! For example, no rational and self-interested person in the original position would agree to enslave all the Norwegian people. Why not? Because if you don't know your own ethnicity, it's just as likely that you are Norwegian! Various forms of oppression, abuse, and discrimination are rejected outright on the grounds that you could potentially be the victim of these crimes. I've often wondered whether police brutality would be reduced if police officers were randomly chosen from the population to serve one-year tours of duty. If you know that the person you're oppressing has an equal chance of being in power next year, it's in your self-interest to treat everyone respectfully.

The procedure of making the worst-off person as best-off as possible is known as the Maximin principle, short for "maximize the minimum." Maximin is often described as pessimistic or safe, because it focuses on improving the worst-case scenario. The strategy usually shows up in the field of decision theory, where a player might use it to make the decision that maximizes her lowest payoff. Since we don't know which role we might be assigned from the original position, Maximin dictates that we maximize the minimum payoff for the *entire set of players*. This is often described as making the worst-off person as best-off as possible. It says that a decision is only justified if it benefits the poorest member of the society.

The political principles that Rawls derives from the original position are focused on improving the welfare of the worst-off people. I won't have much to say about Rawls's political theory in this book, but since this is his most famous contribution to the history of philosophy, it's worth mentioning briefly. In Rawls's approach, rights and opportunities should be distributed to all people, since this clearly improves the situation of the worst-off person. This is both unsurprising and uncontroversial to readers living in liberal democracies. When it comes to political rights, giving more to one group will necessarily take away some from another, so we must distribute them equally to everyone. However, Rawls is not an egalitarian about *wealth*. He acknowledges that there are some possible ways of distributing wealth in a society that make the poorest people better-off than an egalitarian distribution. One reason for this is Rawls's acknowledgement of incentives: people will work harder in situations where there is wealth inequality and social mobility; I will work harder if I know that it will get me a promotion or a raise. This overall increase in productivity raises the level of wealth for the entire society, and thus makes even the poorest people better off than they would have been an egalitarian society. However, Rawls thinks that wealth inequalities are justified *only* to the extent that they make the poorest people better-off, and as soon as wealth inequality becomes greater than necessary for that function, it should be redistributed.[1]

I was once speaking to an enthusiastic free-market capitalist who was surprised to learn that Rawls thinks it's an *empirical* assumption which economic institutions make life best for the poorest people. If it turns out that, as many free-market enthusiasts claim, unrestricted capitalism raises up the poorest people in a society more than any other economic or political system, then Rawls would completely support it. He strongly suspects that this is *not* the case, but the question is completely an economic one rather than a moral one. I do think that Rawls's theory is the correct approach to be using for decisions about political and economic institutions, but because that is not the subject of this book, I'll leave political and economic issues to the side. We are interested in using Rawls's theory for the purpose of individual decision making, and specifically those contexts where autonomous machines might be replacing humans in their capacities.

Players

The question of who counts as an agent and who counts as a patient is essential to any decision procedure. Since Contractarianism arises from optimal moves in cooperation games, moral patients are anything capable of playing a cooperation game. This rules out inanimate objects having any inherent moral value. Cooperation games can only exist between objects that prefer one state to another, so laptops, cars, rocks, mountains, and rivers are not patients. This doesn't mean that they have no value, it just means that they are only valuable because of people who have preferences about them. Contractarianism therefore rejects "ecocentric" moral theories that confer inherent moral value to the environment. There's nothing morally bad about destroying a river if it doesn't have any negative impact on the preferences of moral patients. Of course, destroying rivers and laptops usually *does* have an impact on our preferences.

A more difficult question is whether animals count as players. There's a wide range of disagreement on this topic. On the one side are philosophers like Tom Regan (1973), who extends animals the same moral rights as humans. On the other side are philosophers like John Locke (1689) and Immanuel Kant (1785), who have denied animals any moral standing at all. Locke (1689) argues that humans have rights (and animals don't) because humans have an equal nature, created by God, while other animals are created to be "used" by humans:

> [W]e have the same abilities, and share in one common nature, so there can't be any rank-ordering that would authorize some of us to destroy others, as if we were made to be used by one another, as the lower kinds of creatures are made to be used by us.

If you've read up to this point, you can recognize that this is a terrible argument. Just because a religious text says an action is acceptable doesn't make it so, otherwise slavery and genocide would be morally permissible. Kantians argue against animal rights from a stronger assumption: rights originate from reasoning about means, ends, and contradictions, which animals can't do. Philosopher Carl Cohen (1985) clearly explains why this excludes animals:

> [Animals] are not beings of a kind capable of exercising or responding to moral claims. Animals therefore have no rights, and they can have none … The holders of rights must have the capacity to comprehend rules of duty, governing all including themselves.

Given this range of views, what does Contractarianism have to say about animals? Tom Regan (1973) accuses Rawls of sharing Kant's position on animals. If morality is based on agreement to a contract, then it seems like the only objects to which it applies are rational humans, since they are the only ones capable of understanding a contract and agreeing to it. Regan (1973) writes:

> As for animals [according to Rawls], since they cannot understand contracts, they obviously cannot sign; and since they cannot sign, they have no rights. Like children, however, some animals are the objects of the sentimental interest of others … I have, then, according to [C]ontractarianism, no duty directly to your dog or any other animal, not even the duty not to

cause them pain or suffering; my duty not to hurt them is a duty I have to those people who care about what happens to them. As for other animals, where no or little sentimental interest is present – in the case of farm animals, for example, or laboratory rats – what duties we have grow weaker and weaker, perhaps to vanishing point. The pain and death they endure, though real, are not wrong if no one cares about them.

Similarly, if morality emerges from cooperation problems in humans, then it would seem to only apply to humans. Not merely humans, but adult and fully rational humans. Regan continues his criticism:

> [Contractarianism] systematically denies that we have direct duties to those human beings who do not have a sense of justice – young children, for instance, and many mentally retarded humans. And yet it seems reasonably certain that, were we to torture a young child or a retarded elder, we would be doing something that wronged him or her, not something that would be wrong if (and only if) other humans with a sense of justice were upset.

Regan is mistaken about Contractarianism. Animals, young children, and mentally handicapped people are still capable of entering into cooperation games with adult humans. Cooperation games are defined broadly as situations where there exist mutual improvements from outcomes which self-interested people would rationally choose. This doesn't require that agents be rational, or even conscious of their own preferences, only that they possess genuine interests which can be identified. In a very real sense, plants prefer sunlight to darkness without understanding why, or being conscious of this preference. Contractarianism isn't about the rational agreement that people *actually* make; in fact, many adult humans aren't capable of recognizing what's in their long-term interests. Instead, the original position is based on a *hypothetical* contract: we imagine what it would be like if the entity were granted rationality and put into the original position. It's true that adult humans typically find themselves in cooperation games with other adult humans, and this has been the main historical force behind the evolution of moral grammar. But an argument can be made that farm animals are currently engaged in cooperation games with humans as well. In fact, philosophers Mark Rowlands (1997) and Robert Garner (2013) have both independently argued that Rawls's version of Contractarianism gives animals moral consideration.[2] Rowlands and Garner are correct: animals do indeed possess preferences that can be identified, and thus they should be considered moral patients.

I imagine a critic shouting: "Are you saying that animal lives are just as valuable as human lives, and you'd be willing to sacrifice the life of a human for the life of an animal?" This isn't a trivial question, since we could easily program self-driving cars and military drones to treat animals and humans equally. A driverless vehicle might swerve to avoid killing a deer, predicting that its passengers will only be mildly injured. Attack drones might strike a lightly populated hospital rather than a hill filled with goats. However, none of this follows from the original position. There's an old argument from the philosopher John Stuart Mill (1861) about some states being objectively preferable to others, and this same argument can be applied from the original position to the question of being an animal or being a human. Because anyone, even animals, would prefer a human life to a nonhuman animal life, it's still acceptable to give humans a higher status from within the original position.[3]

Just because humans have a higher status than animals, this doesn't mean they have no moral status at all, as Locke and Kant suggest. Humans are playing cooperation games with animals, so we have a genuine moral obligation to sacrifice nonessential ("luxury") goods to maximize the interests of animals, but not essential ones, since humans are ranked higher than other animals from the original position. If hunting or fishing is the only way of obtaining your health and survival, then this becomes morally acceptable. However, if it's possible to live a life with a normal range of health and opportunity without eating animals (as most people within wealthy societies probably can), this is morally required.

Primary goods

In many cases of actions judged to be wrong, like prostitution, people will project their own cognitive or emotional responses onto the patient, and wind up imagining harm where none really exists (Gray et al., 2014). To move beyond this projection, a moral theory needs to define some objective measurement of when a patient is or isn't harmed, and how much harm is done. The problem is that there is so much disagreement about what counts as harm. Some people are very concerned with physical cleanliness, sexual abstinence, religious obedience, and refraining from consuming things like pork or alcohol. On the other hand, other people don't consider these to be domains of harm at all. The key to resolving this problem is to use the original position. Only goods that everyone would be concerned about count as *moral* goods. Things like physical cleanliness, sexual abstinence, and religious obedience are important for *some* people, but not for others. Rawls refers to these as "secondary goods." These are contrasted with "primary goods," which are goods that are necessary for acquiring anything else, and are therefore desired by everybody.

It's not obvious what counts as a primary good, but there's remarkable convergence on at least a few categories: life, health, opportunity, and essential resources. One of the important features of primary goods is that they are necessary for acquiring any other goods. For instance, it's impossible to write a hit musical or become a successful juggler if you are starving to death or enslaved. And it's hard to do much of anything if you're dead. On the other hand, secondary goods don't prevent you from acquiring other goods. It's completely possible to pursue a life of dirtiness, promiscuity, and atheism while still obtaining televisions and coffee. Many people have led long and happy lives in this condition!

Most harms involve an obvious and unnecessary loss in primary goods. Homicide results in a loss of life, battery results in a loss of health, deception and cheating result in loss of opportunities, and stealing results in a loss of essential resources. For historical convergence on this idea, consider John Locke's list of natural rights from his *Second Treatise of Government* (1689):

> Everyone is obliged to preserve himself and not opt out of life willfully, so for the same reason everyone ought, when his own survival isn't at stake, to do as much as he can to preserve the rest of mankind; and except when it's a matter of punishing an offender, no-one may take away or damage anything that contributes to the preservation of someone else's life, liberty, health, limb, or goods.

Locke's list of rights is similar to Rawls's list of primary goods, and this probably isn't a coincidence. Thinking about what all humans in a natural state of equality would share, Locke was developing an early version of the original position.

It's relatively obvious which actions lead to damage in life and health. But what exactly is a loss or gain in opportunity? It isn't the same as a guarantee; having the opportunity to apply for a job doesn't mean being given the job. Instead, opportunity here is usually synonymous with having a chance to *apply* for the job. To achieve a goal, not only does somebody need the right kind of capacities, but the world also must be arranged so that it's *possible* for the agent to satisfy her goals. If two people apply for the same job, the more qualified person is more likely to get it, even though they both have the same opportunity. This just means that the employer considered everybody's application.

It may be helpful to split the category of "opportunity" into two parts, one having to do with the capacities of the *person*, and the other involving the person's *environment*. In order to pursue any goals, a person must have basic physical and cognitive capacities like perception, motor abilities, the ability to prefer some states to others, and a minimal comprehension of the world around her. These are the typical criteria for being competent to make legal or medical decisions. Any damage to a person's competence is a loss of their opportunity to pursue goals. In addition to competence, opportunity also requires the right kind of environment to be able to pursue a normal range of goals. This includes access to accurate information, freedom of mobility, essential resources, a basic education, and a clean environment. These conditions are almost extensions of basic physical capacities, and Table 4.1 demonstrates those connections.

Following Locke, many libertarians accept people's rights to their physical capacities, but not rights to environmental conditions. However, there's no principled way of drawing the difference between them; one is an extension of the other. If it's wrong to paralyze a person, it's also wrong to keep them locked in a room. If it's wrong to blow harmful smoke in someone's face without their consent, it's also wrong to fill harmful smoke in the air that a person breathes without their consent. If it's wrong to lie to someone, it's also wrong to allow that

68 Contractarianism

TABLE 4.1 A table of necessary conditions for a person to accomplish a normal range of human interests, categorized by states of a person and states of her environment.

Opportunity

Capacities	*Environment*
Perceptual Abilities	Access to Accurate Information
Low-Level Motor Abilities	Unrestricted Mobility
Abilities to Prefer A to B	Essential Material Resources
Minimal Conceptual Competence	Minimal Environmental Protection

person to believe falsehoods without any access to proper sources of evidence and reasoning. The justifications for all these judgments are the same: they are restricting a person's potential to pursue the goals that any human being might want to achieve.

The distinction between primary and secondary goods allows us to determine exactly where moral rules are going to be applicable. Actions that influence the distribution of only secondary goods in a population may fall under social norms and laws, but they don't fall under moral rules. In the original position, I may wind up being someone who desires televisions, or I might wind up being someone who doesn't care about them at all. Decisions about the distribution of televisions are therefore not something that can be decided with the original position method. The only effects of actions that can be measured objectively are the distributions of primary goods, because every person values them equally.

Primary goods solve the problem that moral theories like utilitarianism face when they try to compare one person's happiness to another person's suffering. The technical name for this problem is "intrapersonal comparisons of utility." Consider Peter Singer's (1972) claim that the happiness a rich person gets from buying a $200 pair of shoes is less than the happiness a family gets from $200 worth of medications that save their child's life. This is extremely plausible, even though I don't know how to establish the truth of it besides plausibility. If the rich person insists that she *does* get more happiness from the shoes, I would only give her a shocked stare, and maybe a prod of "Come on!" But there would be nothing else I can say. This gets more obvious when we compare the happiness of one person at the opera to the happiness of another person playing video games. In principle, utilitarianism needs an objective way of measuring happiness, and this has always been a challenge. Contractarianism avoids the challenge entirely by ignoring all other goods besides the ones that are necessary for any person to accomplish a normal range of human goals. Everyone desires and values primary goods equally, because everyone is equally handicapped by their removal. Life and opportunity are equally valuable to the rich and the poor, the young and the old, the sick and the healthy. Essential resources are equally valuable to people of all ethnicities, religions, and occupations. Because of this, we can assume an

Sample Payoff Table

States	P1	P2	P3	P4	P5	P6
A1	30	30	30	30	30	30
A2	99	10	10	10	10	10

FIGURE 4.3 A sample of payoffs in two actions (A1–A2) for six players (P1–P6).

objective standard of value for all the primary goods, and evaluate their effects on people with a wide variety of secondary interests.

In our intuitive moral grammar, primary goods roughly correspond to the element HARM. We saw in the first chapter that people aren't just sensitive to harm, but harm that's *caused* by an agent. This is an important feature that we should incorporate into Contractarianism. It's not only the distributions of primary goods that are important, but the *changes* in how primary goods are distributed. For example, imagine two possible distributions of a primary good like health, where 0 is the worst state of health and 100 is perfect health. These distributions are divided among six people (P1–P6), and caused by Action 1 (A1) or Action 2 (A2), as shown in Figure 4.3.

In the distribution caused by A1, all players get the same amount of health (30). On the other hand, in the distribution caused by A2, the second player gets a large amount of health (90), while the other five get much lower payoffs (10). Which one of these distributions is better? If you're a utilitarian, you might think A1 is better, since it creates more goods overall for more people (180 vs. 140). What about Contractarianism? If all we're looking at is the outcomes, then Contractarians would agree that A1 is best, since it brings the worst-off people to a much better condition (30 vs. 10).

However, this chart is leaving out something very important: the distribution of goods *before* either of these actions was performed. Call this the prior distribution. Imagine that, before either A1 or A2 is performed, Player 1 previously had a large amount of health (90), while all the other players had very low amounts (5). Many of your intuitions might change dramatically here. Before, you might have said: "Why should Player 1 get all that benefit, while those other players get so much less?" But now, there's a sense in which Player 1 *isn't* benefitting from either of these actions, but all the other players are. This sense of "benefit" defines goods not just by the end-result but by how much each person has *gained or lost*, and this is the sense of benefit that a Contractarian should be using. Even from behind a veil of ignorance, the amount of goods that are gained or lost is something that all humans value, rather than just the final distributions. There's no reason that people wouldn't have access to the prior distributions as well as the future ones, and I don't see any way for a Rawlsian to dismiss them. If we are measuring not only payoffs of primary goods but also the changes in distributions of primary goods, then the calculation will be:

$$[\text{change in primary goods}] = [\text{expected state}] - [\text{prior state}]$$

Sample Payoff Table (expanded)

States	P1	P2	P3	P4	P5	P6
Prior	90	5	5	5	5	5
A1	30	30	30	30	30	30
A2	99	10	10	10	10	10
Changes from A1	**−60**	25	25	25	25	25
✓ Changes from A2	9	**5**	5	5	5	5

FIGURE 4.4 Changes in primary goods. The rows in gray are the payoffs for each player in A1 and A2, and the rows below them are the expected changes that these payoffs produce from the prior distribution of goods.

Performing this operation on our example here gives a dataset that we can call the *changes* from A1 and A2 (Figure 4.4).

Using the bottom two rows, utilitarianism and Contractarianism will now disagree about which action is better. While A1 creates more overall happiness for more people (the sum is 65 compared to 16), A2 now improves the condition of the worst-off person (5 compared to −60). This is an important aspect of Contractarianism: it's wrong to make one person's conditions worse off to improve the conditions of other people.

In case you're worried that I'm now defining the wealthiest people in a society as the worst-off because they have more to lose, remember that these are measurements of *primary goods* like health and essential resources, not luxuries and wealth. Distributing wealth from rich to poor is very different from distributing health, opportunities, or liberties. In fact, excess wealth beyond essential resources is not a primary good, so from a Contractarian perspective, it's not even morally relevant. This may imply that distributing wealth from the rich to the poor is *not* morally wrong at all, so long as it doesn't lead to any violence or restrictions in opportunities. This may sound strange, but it's part of one of the most important questions in political philosophy: why is it acceptable for a state to disproportionately tax the rich more than the poor, and provide the poor with more subsidies? Assuming that whatever is legal should also be morally acceptable, this turns out to be a fortunate result for anyone interested in even the most minimal role in a government providing subsidies to the poor.

Maximin

Rawls thinks that, from the original position, all rational and self-interested people would use the decision-making rule: *maximize the worst-off outcome* (Maximin) But why would people agree to this rule, and not another one, like *maximize the best-off outcome* (Maximax) or *maximize the sum of outcomes* (Maxisum)?

One answer is internal to the original position method: if you don't have information about the distribution of goods in a population, or the *number of people* in the population, it will be in your self-interest to maximize the minimum.

According to standard decision theory, the best rule for a self-interested agent to make choices with is something we can call the *expected value rule*. To illustrate the rule, imagine that I have a game where you can roll a normal six-sided die for a chance to win some money. The game costs $10 to play, and if it lands on 4, you win $120. If it lands on any of the other five sides, you get nothing. Is it a good idea to play this game? Through informal polling of students, friends, and very annoyed people at parties, I've found that some are willing to play this game and others aren't. Many people think that there's no objective way of answering whether it's a good idea to play. As a waiter once told me, "It's a game of chance." This is the same kind of reasoning that leads people to play the state lottery; one recent motto is: "Somebody's gotta win!"

Unfortunately, both these inferences are invalid, and can be financially dangerous. Lotteries are almost always *objectively bad* ideas to play, and the dice game that I described above happens to be an *objectively good* idea to play. To see why, consider your two possible choices: play or don't play. The expected value of not playing the game is just the money you would save, which is the cost of the game: $10. The expected value of playing is more complicated. There are six possible outcomes, and each have an equal 1/6 probability. In one outcome (rolling 4), you get $120, while in the other five, you get $0. To find the total expected value, multiply the likelihood of each outcome (1/6) by its payoff, and add them all up (Figure 4.5). This will give an expected value for playing the game of $20. Since the expected value of playing is higher than the value of not playing, it's the better choice. A good way of thinking about this is to imagine playing the game repeatedly over time. You keep paying $10, and on average, you win $120 once every six games, even though you lose the $10 in the other five out of six games. If this keeps going, you'll make small amounts of money slowly over time, even if you're losing most of your games. This is the expected value rule: find the value of an action by summing all its potential payoffs, discounted by the probabilities of each payoff.

The economist John Harsanyi (1975) argued that, if we're self-interested from within the original position, then we should be using the expected value rule. This argument is sound. However, Harsanyi also thought that the expected value rule

Derek's Dice Game

	1	2	3	4	5	6	Value
Play Game	$(\frac{1}{6})$\$0	$(\frac{1}{6})$\$0	$(\frac{1}{6})$\$0	$(\frac{1}{6})$\$120	$(\frac{1}{6})$\$0	$(\frac{1}{6})$\$0	**$20**
Don't Play							**$10**

FIGURE 4.5 A dice game which costs $10 to play, where you win $120 for rolling a 4, and $0 for rolling anything else. Find the expected value by multiplying each outcome by its probability (1/6), and adding them up. Since playing has double the expected value than not playing, it's the rational choice.

72 Contractarianism

Reverse Russian Roulette

	P1	P2	P3	P4	P5	P6	E. Value
A1	$(\frac{1}{6})$ 0	$(\frac{1}{6})$ 0	$(\frac{1}{6})$ 0	$(\frac{1}{6})$ 120	$(\frac{1}{6})$ 0	$(\frac{1}{6})$ 0	20
A2	$(\frac{1}{6})$ 10	$(\frac{1}{6})$ 10	$(\frac{1}{6})$ 10	$(\frac{1}{6})$ 10	$(\frac{1}{6})$ 10	$(\frac{1}{6})$ 10	10

FIGURE 4.6 Two possible distributions of goods: in A1, five players get nothing and one player gets a large amount (120), while in A2, each player gets an equally small amount (10). Harsanyi's Maxisum rule picks A1, while Rawls's Maximin rule picks A2.

will lead to something more like maximizing the sum of outcomes (Maxisum), rather than maximizing the minimum (Maximin), which I don't think necessarily follows. This would lead to a kind of utilitarianism, although not exactly the standard variety, since it's only calculating which action maximizes the total sum of primary goods rather than all pleasures and pains. Harsanyi's reasoning initially looks solid. Imagine that there is a population of six people, and two possible distributions of goods: give everybody 10 units, or give one person 120 units, while all the other players get nothing. Call this game Reverse Russian Roulette, since you're pulling the trigger on a six-chambered gun, hoping to get the bullet (Figure 4.6). In this game, just like my dice game, Rawls's Maximin principle leads to an equal distribution in this situation, while Harsanyi's Maxisum principle produces the unequal one. But Harsanyi's case appears strong: if we agree that the expected value rule is correct for the dice game, doesn't it also suggest that a rational agent in the original position would take a chance on being the lucky player?

I don't think it does. In the situation above, we have access not only to the payoffs that people receive, but also the *number of people* who receive each payoff. For example, we can see that six people in A1 receive 10, while five people in A2 receive 0. However, Rawls insists that people should *not* have access to this information from within the original position. He calls this a "thick" version of the veil of ignorance. Without knowledge of the total number of outcomes, it's impossible to assign a probability. It could turn out that in A2 there are five people with 0, or five million. Without this information, Rawls suggests that playing it safe with Maximin is the most self-interested principle.

Within the theory, there's some reason to prefer this "thick" version of the veil of ignorance. The purpose of the veil is to put a person in a position where they say: "*I could really be anyone!*" In other words, you have an equal probability of being any person. If this is true, then every person's self-interest will be identical, and their decisions will be perfectly cooperative. However, if you know that there are 50 people in a society and only one of them is paralyzed, then it doesn't accomplish the goal of perfect cooperative behavior through pure anonymity. The point isn't to say: "I have a 2 percent chance of being paraplegic," but instead, "I *have no idea* what my chances are of being paraplegic." All you know from the original position is that at least one person is disabled, but it could be just one person or the vast majority of the population. This would ensure maximal cooperation between able and disabled people, since their interests literally become identical. All of this being said, I'll describe in the next chapter how Harsanyi was correct that numbers of people with each payoff can become important even within a thick original position, but this only occurs in special cases where we are weighing equal losses against each other.

This defense of the Maximin principle is theory-internal, but recall that entities like the veil of ignorance are nothing more than tools created for producing cooperative behavior. It should therefore be possible to step outside the theory and make a *theory-external* comparison between Rawls's and Harsanyi's principles based on their success in producing cooperative behavior. I mentioned above that the expected value rule leads to a version of utilitarianism, and as we've seen in the previous chapter, utilitarianism fails to produce cooperative behavior in games like the Repugnant Prisoner's Dilemma. Maximin is simply a better rule for producing cooperative behavior. Maximin will produce cooperative behavior in every game we've described (you can test this for yourself). In fact, a complete version of the Maximin rule that I will elaborate in the next chapter (called "Leximin") will produce cooperative behavior in any cooperation game, using the definitions that we've been employing. It also generalizes to dilemma situations like Reverse Russian Roulette and the Trolley Problem. Because Maximin succeeds where theories like utilitarianism and libertarianism fail, I propose that it is the optimal moral principle, and the one we should be using to resolve moral conflicts.

There's still more to be done in explaining Contractarianism, but these are the nuts and bolts of the theory. In Chapter 5, I'll say more about how each of these components should be defined and quantified. Only after these details are complete can we apply the theory to real-world decisions. But we're now at a stage where it's possible to move from justifying the moral theory to showing how it can be implemented in machines.

Chapter summary

- Contractarianism is a theory based on abstracting from cooperation problems into an ideal solution space called the "original position," and it is thus well poised to provide advantages that other moral theories may lack. Just like all the other moral theories, the entities within Contractarianism aren't "real," but they are tools invented for reaching new solutions to cooperation problems that might not have been possible previously.
- The basic components of Contractarianism are: (1) a set of self-interested players, (2) a set of primary goods that are equally valued by all the players, and (3) a principle for choosing from among possible distributions of primary goods called Maximin.
- Self-interested players are any objects that have genuine preferences and find themselves in cooperation games with each other. This includes nonhuman animals, although an argument from John Stuart Mill can be plausibly made

that species distinctions are the kind of things that all agents would care about from the original position.
- Primary goods are the states that all agents from the original position equally care about maximizing. This includes: life, opportunity, health, and essential resources. There are objective ways of quantifying distributions of these goods. Distributions should also be measured as a difference from each agent's *current state*, so that two players could both wind up with 50 units of some good, but one player is worse-off if she started off with more units than the other player.
- The Maximin principle is a way of selecting distributions of primary goods based on making the worst-off player as best-off as possible (or, "maximizing the minimum"). Rawls and Harsanyi disagreed about whether this would be the rational decision procedure to use for a self-interested agent from the original position. Harsanyi was correct that expected value theory generates a utilitarian distribution rule if we have access to population data from the original position (a "thin" original position). Rawls was correct that expected value theory predicts the Maximin rule, if we don't have access to that data (a "thick" original position). Stepping into theory-external evaluations, we should prefer the thick original position, since the rule that it generates will always produce cooperative behavior.

Notes

1 In *A Theory of Justice*, Rawls seems to suggest that the difference principle can be directly derived from the Maximin principle, but in his later work, he claims that additional reasons are needed to justify it. It seems to me that the difference principle *does* follow directly from Maximin, but since all of Rawls's additional arguments for it are based on greater cooperation amongst self-interested parties, this doesn't influence anything in the present discussion.
2 Extending Contractarianism to farm animals implies clean and healthy conditions which benefit animals, in exchange for animal products that benefit the farmer. If animals have no strong preferences about whether their milk and eggs are taken, or whether they are butchered in a painless way after leading a pleasant life, this might also fit in to a cooperative agreement. The basic idea of Pareto-optimality is that a good solution makes life better for each party than it would have otherwise been, while avoiding the problems of either one taking advantage of the other. It's plausible that a life for an animal on a free-range farm where it is treated well and humanely killed is a better life than it would have had in the wild. That being said, farmers still have moral obligations to make life at least as pleasant for animals as it would be for them in the wild, while also securing the highest benefits for themselves (in accordance with Maximin).

If you take the idea of "superintelligence" seriously, this is a happy result. By superintelligence, I mean an artificial intelligence that goes far beyond the capacities of any humans alive today. In his book, *Superintelligence* (2014), philosopher Nick Bostrom outlines several different potential routes to this situation. There is widespread disagreement about the likelihood and time line of a superintelligence being created, but Bostrom urges us to take the idea seriously. If humans find themselves engaged in cooperation with a superintelligence at some point in the future, this intelligence will be to us what we are currently to nonhuman animals. It's certainly a benefit if the optimal solution to cooperation problems is to take seriously the well-being of the other party, despite their cognitive limitations. We wouldn't need to worry about a superintelligence putting us in human free-range farms, since we (unlike animals) have strong preferences about the long-term shape of our lives, including the way we die. A superintelligence acting according to Contractarianism would need to respect these preferences as well (or put us in a virtual reality free-range farm, like *The Matrix*, where we don't know that we're in a farm).

3 The argument for this position is provided by John Stuart Mill in the first few pages of his classic text, *Utilitarianism* (1861). Mill denies that the pleasures of pigs are equal to the "pleasures of the intellect" that humans enjoy. Instead there are differences between "higher" pleasures of humans and "lower" pleasures of animals. He defines a higher pleasure as one that all (or "almost all") people would prefer, after having experienced both. Even though Contractarianism isn't based on pleasures and pains, it is based on interests, and an argument can be made that the totality of interests in a human life is preferable to the totality of interests in an animal life. Preferable to whom? As Mill argues, to those who have experienced both. A racist person might say that a European life is more valuable than an Asian life, but Rawls predicts that if you had an equal chance of being European or Asian, and you had enough knowledge of what each life is like, you would agree that each life is equally valuable. None of us has the experience of being a nonhuman animal, but we certainly share a number of their "base" experiences, and have enough knowledge about what their lives are like. Importantly, this isn't a claim about the kinds of capacities that animals have, it's a claim about what preferences a person would have with an equal chance of being a human or an animal. I predict that anyone with enough experience of animal life and human life would still prefer the totality of human interests over nonhuman animal interests, and would rank human primary goods over animal primary goods.

References

Bostrom, Nick (2014). *Superintelligence: Paths, Dangers, Strategies*. Oxford: Oxford University Press.

Cohen, Carl (1985). "The Case for the Use of Animals in Biomedical Research." *New England Journal of Medicine*, 315, 865–870.

Garner, Robert (2013). *A Theory of Justice for Animals: Animal Rights in a Nonideal World*. Oxford: Oxford University Press.

Gray, Kurt & Schein, Chelsea & Ward, Adrian (2014). "The Myth of Harmless Wrongs in Moral Cognition: Automatic Dyadic Completion from Sin to Suffering." *Journal of Experimental Psychology: General*, 143, 1600–1615.

Harsanyi, John (1975). "Can the Maximin Principle Serve as a Basis for Morality? A critique of John Rawls' theory." *The American Political Science Review*, 69.

Kant, Immanuel (1785). *Groundwork on the Metaphysics of Morals*. Cambridge: Cambridge University Press.

Locke, John (1689). *Second Treatise of Government*. New York: Hackett.

Mill, John Stuart (1861). *Utilitarianism*. New York: Hackett.

Rawls, John (1971). *A Theory of Justice*. Cambridge, MA: Harvard University Press.

Regan, Tom (1973). *The Case for Animal Rights*. Berkeley, CA: University of California Press.

Rowlands, Mark (1997). "Contractarianism and Animal Rights." *Journal of Applied Philosophy*, 14, 225–247.

Singer, Peter (1972). "Famine, Affluence, and Morality." *Philosophy and Public Affairs*, 1, 229–243.

5
ETHICS ENGINES

In 1770, the Hungarian inventor Wolfgang Von Kempelen revealed his Mechanical Turk, a machine that could supposedly play chess and win against even the most skilled human players. Von Kempelen toured the machine around Europe and America for decades, amazing large audiences and defeating the likes of Napoleon Bonaparte and Benjamin Franklin. Edgar Allen Poe called it "the most astonishing of the inventions of mankind."

Unfortunately, it was later revealed that the machine was a fraud; a chess master secretly hid behind the elaborate gears, controlling the movements of the machine (Figure 5.1). It turns out that a chess-playing machine *can* be created, but it wouldn't be until the second half of the twentieth century that Alan Turing and Claude Shannon would independently develop real chess-playing machines. Now, more than 60 years later, most personal computers come equipped with a chess program that can play at a level that Von Kempelen could only dream of. It's not crazy to think that the same thing can happen with ethics, and it might be useful to think about how chess engines work when designing our ethics engine.

Chess programs typically have the following components: (1) a representation of the pieces and their locations, (2) a map of all the possible moves and outcomes, (3) some way of assigning a value to each outcome, and (4) a strategy rule that will lead to a unique decision (Figure 5.2).

For example, on the first move, a chess program will represent the current board state and map out the 20 possible moves for white. Then it will map out the state of the board from those outcomes, and all the possible moves for black. We can depict this map as a tree, where every node in the tree is a state of the board, and every branch is a move that leads to a new state.[1] After mapping out a sufficiently large tree of moves, the chess engine will assign a value to each

Ethics engines

FIGURE 5.1 A copper engraving of Von Kempelen's chess-playing robot, The Mechanical Turk, from a 1783 book by Karl Gottlieb von Windisch.

node on the tree. One simple way of assigning a value to each board state would be to count who has more pieces on the board. But this would be too simple for chess, since some pieces are more important than others. In his 1950 chess program, Shannon evaluated board states by using coefficients to weight the different pieces, where bishops and knights are three times more valuable than a pawn, a rook is five times more valuable than a pawn, and a queen is nine times more valuable than a pawn.[2]

Now let's think about how an ethics engine would work. Just like a chess engine, it will represent all the relevant objects within the current state, map out possible actions and outcomes, assign a value to each outcome, and then use a rule for picking which action is best. Each of these steps involves important moral assumptions. What are the relevant objects and actions? How do we assign numerical values to each outcome? What is the best rule for making a decision? Fortunately, the first half of this book has provided us with all the theoretical work needed to answer these questions. In the first half, I argued for the use of Contractarianism as a moral theory. Contractarianism states that actions are morally acceptable whenever they would be chosen by a self-interested agent from a position where she could (for all she knows) wind up being anyone in the society. Moral decisions always involve the distribution of primary goods (life, health, opportunity, and essential resources) according to the Maximin rule. More specifically, we'll use a modified version of Maximin, called *Leximin*. We'll also add a role for consent in updating

78 Ethics engines

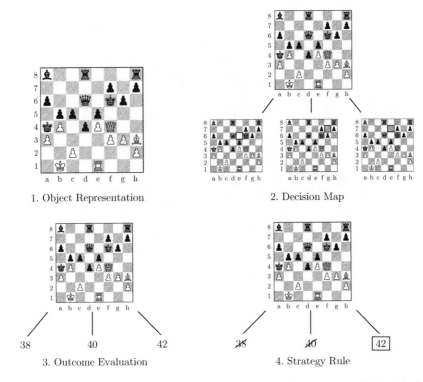

FIGURE 5.2 A simplified picture of a chess engine. First, the program will identify the current state and all the possible moves. Then it will assign a value to each of the outcomes, and use a decision rule to select a unique move. This is simplified because I'm showing a state where there are only three possible moves for black, we're only going one level deep into future outcomes, and I'm using a "pick the highest value" rule. The board state is from Kasparov vs. Topalov (1999).

or confirming preference rankings. Using Contractarianism, we can fill in all the details needed for an ethics engine:

1. Object representation: The current state of all the players and their primary goods.
2. Decision map: The available actions and their likely (predicted) outcomes in primary goods.
3. Outcome evaluation: The difference between each player's current state of primary goods and their predicted state of primary goods (for each action).
    3.5. Consensual updating or confirmation of preference rankings.
4. Strategy rule: Leximin.

Consider an example with two players, Sean and Ethan, along with three possible actions. The first step would represent the players and their prior state of primary goods; let's say that Ethan has 12 units and Sean has 34 units. The next step of an ethics engine considers all the possible moves an agent can make from

Ethics engines **79**

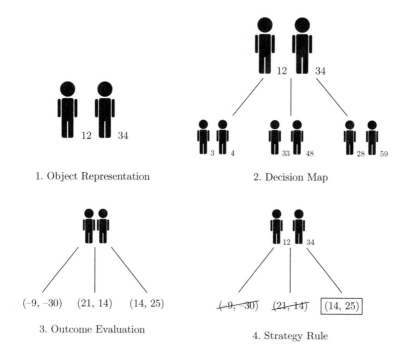

FIGURE 5.3 An ethics engine modeled after a chess engine.

its current position, and the outcomes it will produce. Say that the first action will produce a distribution of: (3, 4), the second produces a distribution of: (33, 48), and the third produces a distribution of: (28, 59). The third step will assign some numerical values to each state by calculating the arithmetic difference in primary goods for each player: (–9, 30), (21, 14), and (14, 25). At this point, there is an optional role for consent in updating or confirming these payoffs for each player. In a simple version, a machine could check with each player to confirm their ordinal rankings, asking Player 1: "Is it true that you prefer B to C, and C to A?" If these payoffs are reliable, our Maximin decision procedure will pick the third action as winner (Figure 5.3).

There are serious engineering challenges in designing an ethics engine, but most of them will be ignored here. The philosophical challenge is identifying what information we're using to fill in the open places, called the *parameters* of the model. It's important to specify the parameters, since a program won't be useful if we put the wrong information into it. As computer scientists are fond of saying, "garbage in, garbage out." Before using the ethics engine, we need to identify what information will be used for players and quantities of primary goods.

The players parameter: avoiding discrimination

Any robot equipped with an ethics engine must be capable of recognizing humans and distinguishing them from other physical objects. But what additional information should it use in representing humans? Should a machine be capable of distinguishing specific categories of humans based on age, gender, race, sexual orientation, or beliefs? Initially this seems like a bad idea. After all, treating people differently on the basis of the group they belong to might be the definition of discrimination. Doesn't Rawls claim that the veil of ignorance prevents us from caring about this information from an ethical point of view? In one sense, this is true, since we must assume that we could be a member of *any* social group, and thus ignore that information. On the other hand, demographic facts can sometimes be relevant in assessing the distribution of primary goods. For example, an older person might be less likely to survive a car crash than a younger person, so it might be useful for a driverless vehicle to detect the age and size of pedestrians. But how do we know what type of demographic information should or shouldn't be represented?

According to Contractarianism, any categories that have some influence on the distribution of primary goods are relevant to an ethics engine. For example, a person's age and size are relevant to the distribution of health, but not their religion or sexual orientation. Most of the time, the properties that have some impact on the distribution of primary goods will be physical properties of the person: their age, sex, size, and biological functioning. The person's location will also be very important, and when a driverless vehicle categorizes some people as *pedestrians* and others as *passengers*, this is just a physical fact that one of them happens to be located inside a vehicle and the other person is outside. The properties that are unlikely to influence a person's distribution of primary goods are social facts that depend on their relationship to other people: religion, race, nationality, sexual orientation, personality, intelligence, occupation, economic class, and political attitudes. In fact, using these categories to make decisions about people's lives will inevitably lead machines down the road to unfair discrimination.

It's worth briefly reminding ourselves about why discrimination is a bad thing. Just in terms of statistical reasoning, it's invalid to use generalizations about group membership to make predictions about individual members of that group. Even if there is a higher average level of performance in one group, there can be so much variance between groups that using social categories to make predictions about individuals will often be useless. For example, even if ice fishing is more popular among Norwegians than Italians, there is so much variation in the preferences for ice fishing that it's a weak inference to say: "Carla is Norwegian, so she probably loves ice fishing." Because this is a book about ethics, the more interesting argument against discrimination is a moral one: there's something *dehumanizing* about using information about a person's group membership to make predictions about his or her behavior, even if this prediction turns out to be correct. I'm sure most readers have had the experience of someone telling them, "Oh, you're [social category], you must like/do/think [x]." There's something offensive about this, even when it's true. The statistical argument shows why profiling is an invalid inference, but the moral argument shows why it's something blameworthy.

The original position method can explain what's offensive about profiling: there's something disrespectful about not considering a person as an individual, but *only* as a member of a group. People often describe this experience as being "treated like a statistic." In some of Rawls's later work, he focused on the importance of *respect as an individual*. It's essential for any human's interests that her life is somehow distinguishable from the lives of other humans. If one person is indistinguishable as an individual, then it's impossible for any of her projects to be possible *as her own*. Therefore, this qualifies as a primary good just as much as life, opportunity, and essential resources. Terms like "respect" and "dignity" are vague, but there are ways of being more specific if we contrast this good with being treated as a random member of a group who can be exchanged for another group member without any loss. Using properties like age, size, and biological sex to make predictions about a person does not count as discrimination, because these are intrinsic physical features of an individual that don't involve relations to others. However, using properties like gender and race are disrespectful because they fail to consider a person as an individual.

In 2016, a group of researchers at an Oxford conference entitled "Social Robotics and AI" presented a set of guidelines for ethical behavior in robots. These guidelines, titled "Guide to the Ethical Design and Application of Robotics and Robotic Systems," are typically vague and unhelpful, expressing the usual *don't harm humans* rule that fails to specify what counts as harm and what to do when every action leads to harm. However, the guidelines do indicate a new and important concern about robot discrimination, under the title of "lack of respect for cultural diversity or pluralism." In interviews with *The Guardian* (September 18, 2016), two of the authors, Alan Winfield and Noel Sharkey, note how police and medical robots trained on human judgments alone might "absorb" human prejudices in race, gender, and other relational facts.[3] This is a real problem, and an important reason why we need an ethics engine rather than just training machines to act like humans. However, the solution to preventing discrimination in robots isn't in regulating their decisions. Instead, it comes from restricting the type of information that their moral decision making has *access* to. If we limit this information to physical facts about players rather than social facts about them, then discrimination can be prevented.

What about animals? The previous chapter argued for including nonhuman animals in the category of moral patients, but at a lower ranking than humans. This can be formalized by setting up tiers of players, with humans ranked higher than animals, and animals ranked higher than objects. We only want to make sure that the *primary* goods of humans are never sacrificed for the sake of animals. One way of ensuring this is to only measure the primary goods of animals when there's no loss in primary goods for humans. Essentially, animals are treated like physical objects whenever there's a chance of humans losing their lives, health, opportunity, or essential resources. In outcomes where there's *no* potential loss of primary goods for humans, then animal welfare becomes relevant. Even when animals aren't assigned any payoffs, they still need to be represented.

The outcomes parameter: setting a utility function

Chess engines use an evaluation function to assign numerical values to each outcome. If the ethics engine is going to work, we'll need to assign numbers to every distribution of health, opportunity, and essential resources. It might seem impossible to turn entities like *health* or *opportunity* into a numerical representation, and I imagine that this is where the most skepticism will arise. But this is a challenge that must be overcome in designing an ethical robot. If we can't measure primary goods, there's absolutely no way for machines to make moral decisions, or humans to make them, for that matter.

If it's possible to rank outcomes according to probability of survival, these probabilities can serve as numerical values for measurements of life and health. For example, being hit by a car moving at 50mph produces a lower probability of survival than being hit by the same car moving at 10mph, all else being equal. We can think about these probabilities as degrees of confidence based on frequencies in the available data. If only one out of 100 people (of similar age and size) survives the first scenario, but 95 similar people survive the second, then a computer could easily assign a 1 percent chance of survival in the first case and a 95 percent chance in the second case, with a degree of confidence based on the similarity in a feature-space between the people and scenarios. Equipped with large enough databases about harmful incidents like shootings and poisonings, along with information about how many of these cases are fatal, a machine could assign a probability of survival to being shot versus being poisoned. This provides a concrete answer to questions like "Which is worse, being shot or poisoned?" Importantly, we're not asking: "Which would you prefer?" but instead, "Which is worse for your health?" If there are objective answers to that question, which there must be, then it's possible to give reliable estimates with a large enough database.

Even if you grant that it's possible to quantitatively estimate an action's effects on health, you might be skeptical about doing the same thing with *opportunity*. In the previous chapter, I introduced a list of conditions needed to pursue even the most minimal kinds of interests (Table 4.1). These include access to information, mobility, psychological competence, environmental protection, and essential resources. But how do we *measure* exactly how much a condition is restricting the capacity to perform normal activities? One potential solution comes from considering our judgments about when a group is *underrepresented* in institutions like universities, companies, and governments. If women make up half the population outside a university, but only 1 percent of the faculty in a university, this strongly suggests that women's opportunities are being restricted. This isn't always true, since underrepresentation could be due to some statistical anomaly or other factors unrelated to gender. However, if we take a large and diverse sample of human activities and find that the percentage of women is consistently lower than 50 percent (this is called the *base rate* of how many women are in the population), it strongly suggests that being female restricts one's opportunity in an institution or a society.

I've argued that robots should be unable to detect social-relational properties like race, gender, and sexual orientation. But underrepresentation measurements could also be applied to physical and environmental disabilities. Imagine that we create a large and diverse sample of typical human activities. The sample might include: having a family, owning a home, getting a college degree, going out with friends, and having a career (lawyer, juggler, dancer, barista, etc.). Now let's say we want to know how much one's opportunities are generally restricted by damage to a psychological capacity like visual perception. An underrepresentation measurement would compare the rate of blind people in our sample with their base rate in the population. If blind people make up 0.01 percent of the general population, but only 0.001 percent of our sample, this suggests that blindness restricts one's opportunities by 10 percent. The same method applies to environmental harms; if 30 percent of people in the population lack a basic education, but only 3 percent of them show up in our sample, this suggests that a lack of education restricts a person's opportunities as much as physical blindness. Like any estimate, using underrepresentation data is crude and imperfect.[4] But it provides a relevant numerical evaluation that matches some well-supported assumptions about when *and how much* a condition tends to restrict opportunities. Taken together, the measurements of life and liberty are enough to prevent robots from participating in homicide, battery, threats and intimidation, kidnapping, and most actions that people view to be normally wrong in normal situations.

For outcomes that cause a change in many categories of primary goods, how do we integrate these changes into a single value? If we had some coefficient describing exactly how much a player values one domain over the other, we could integrate these values together as a weighted sum. However, no such coefficient exists. Different people assign different weights to their losses in health, opportunity, liberty, privacy, and essential resources, and sometimes inconsistently across different domains. One person is willing to accept random police searches in exchange for a decrease in the rate of violent terrorist attacks, while another person thinks this violation of privacy isn't a society worth living in. There's nothing irrational about these disagreements, since self-interested and fully informed people can still have different preferences over trade-offs between security and liberty. These preferences are the result of subjective facts about people's personalities, making them inaccessible from within the original position. This looks like trouble for our ethics engine.

Before you skeptically throw this book into the fireplace, there is still one trick up the Contractarian's sleeve. We applied the Maximin procedure to resolve conflicts *between* individual preferences, when we didn't have any information about our subjective preferences. I don't see any reason why we couldn't also apply the Maximin procedure to resolve conflicts *within* an individual's preferences, since these are also based on subjective facts that are inaccessible from behind the veil of ignorance. Every person, no matter what her interests are, values life, liberty, and essential resources. However, not everybody values them *equally*, or more than secondary goods like smoking and plane travel. This means that, if we don't know whether a particular person values life over opportunity in a certain context, we must pick the action with the highest minimum payoff in either category. A robot should be able to restrict a person's mobility to save their life, or slightly injure a person to free them from a kidnapper. The justification for both actions is the same: loss to one category of primary goods is less than the loss to another.

Importantly, every measurement of primary goods must allow updates by the players themselves. This is the role of consent in our theory. If a player conveys that she *prefers* the losses in primary goods that go along with some outcome, then her payoffs must be updated to reflect that wish. This is especially important when the player is the worst-off person (or, equivalently, when nobody else is significantly affected by the action). To illustrate, here is a scenario that might occur without consensual updating:

> You go in to the local gas station, and ask the robot clerk for a pack of cigarettes. The robot refuses. You ask again, but the robot politely explains: "I'm sorry, but selling you cigarettes reduces the likelihood of your survival by 0.00004 percent. Therefore, this action is restricted by my ethics engine."

According to the overly simple *don't harm humans* rule, any action that results in a reduction of survival probability would be unacceptable. This example shows that it's also overly simple to apply an equal value to primary goods across different people. It's important for the ethics engine to set *default* values based on the original position (all primary goods are weighted equally and primary goods are more valuable than secondary goods). However, these defaults can and must be updated based on information about an actual player's preferences.

The role of consent: beyond "I have read and agreed to the terms of service"

As described in a 2013 article of *The Economist*, of the three billion people who flew commercial flights that year, only 210 died. That means the probability of dying in a commercial plane crash is somewhere around 0.00000007 percent. Most of us willingly accept this slight decrease in our probability of survival in exchange for the benefits in mobility that plane travel allows. Even if the chance of dying in a plane crash were to increase by *100 times*, it would still be around the same chance of dying from driving a vehicle around any U.S. city. But let's imagine that the chance of dying in a plane crash were to increase to something insane like 1 percent. Would you still fly in a commercial plane? I probably wouldn't accept such a significant risk of death for plane travel, but how would I criticize someone who did? All I could say is: "I wouldn't do that," but I also know full well that some people are riskier than others. I maintain that, from a Contractarian moral theory, there's no way of criticizing people's risky behavior. Obviously, I can criticize it as being stupid and impractical, but not morally wrong. The same applies to American football players in the NFL, who are now fully aware that playing professional football will increase their chance of Alzheimer's disease by 4 percent, compared to the national average. I don't see this sacrifice as worth the benefits, but others might, and the original position forces me to respect their decisions, even if I wouldn't make that choice.

Consent is one of the central concepts in ethics, and is especially relevant for decisions in the domains of medicine, sex, and business. Utilitarianism tends to place less emphasis on consent, seeing it as valuable only as a tool for creating more overall happiness. Other moral theories view consent as something inherently valuable. Contractarianism views *preferences* as the things that have value, and since consent is a sufficient condition for determining preferences, it will always take precedence over default assumptions. From the original position, we might predict that someone will value their health over the pleasures of smoking cigarettes. However, once a person explicitly says that they prefer cigarettes over their own health, that person's updated preference ranking immediately becomes: "cigarette smoking > long-term health."

The reason why consent must be an optional "updating" step within our ethics engine is that many decisions do not allow time for confirming the preferences of all the people affected. Most bioethicists concede that the policies for *emergency medicine* can be different from the policies for normal medical decision making. Even if respecting a patient's wish to die for religious reasons is acceptable when the patient has the time to make the decision, a doctor must prioritize saving the patient's life in emergency situations. This also applies to autonomous vehicles, which will almost certainly never have the time to consult with pedestrians or passengers about their preferences before a collision, so it would be pointless to expect them to provide consent. Other machines, like medical robots, *will* have time to consult with patients before making a treatment decision. And we all want medical robots to consult with patients before performing surgery.

Assuming there is sufficient time to confirm each player's preferences, an ethics engine must do so. But how can a machine, or a human for that matter, confirm a person's genuine preferences? One simple method is verbal or written confirmation. This is the method used by companies in their notorious "I have read and agreed to the terms of service" box. The joke about these boxes is that nobody ever reads the terms and conditions of service, they just click the box. In ethics, this is the problem of "competence." A patient can agree to a medical treatment, but this doesn't reflect her genuine preference if she is forced into the agreement or doesn't understand what she's agreeing to. Thus, an ethics engine, when there is enough time to do so, must be equipped with some method of determining not only agreement, but also volition and competence. As noted by the bioethicists Buchannan and Brock (1989), all of these measurements must be relative to the importance of the decision, where very important decisions require a higher threshold of competence than unimportant ones. A very general procedure for this part of the ethics engine looks like the following:

Consent procedure

IF there is enough time to confirm a player's preferences,

> THEN, proportionally to the potential losses to that player,
>
>> Confirm the player's preferences via verbal, written, or implied agreement
>>
>> AND check whether another player is forcing this agreement
>>
>> AND check whether the player has any general impairments in her decision making (being a minor, being intoxicated, being cognitively impaired, etc.)
>>
>> AND measure whether the patient's knowledge crosses a minimal threshold for the relevant domain.

There are many factors that can universally impair decision making in every domain, like being a child, being intoxicated, and being cognitively impaired. There exist fairly standardized and reliable measurements for each of these impairments, and they should each be administered, relative to the importance of the decision. In addition to these general standards for competence, a player must also possess a minimal knowledge about the relevant domain. For example, if I'm making a decision about which cancer treatment I prefer, the doctor treating me needs to ensure that I understand what cancer is, what its effects are for my particular type and stage, as well as the major treatment options and each of their "pros and cons." It doesn't matter if I lack concepts about planes, trains, and automobiles, since these domains are completely irrelevant to the decision at hand. To establish that a patient possesses the relevant knowledge about some domain, human doctors usually employ informal conversations with the patient and use their intuitive judgments. Sophisticated robots might be able to do the same thing, if they are trained on a large database of expert judgments about who is informed in a particular area. However, actual exams for competence can conceivably be administered, depending on the importance of the decision. For buying cigarettes, a robotic clerk might conceivably ask: "True or false: cigarette smoking increases the risk of lung disease, emphysema, and birth defects."

As Buchannan and Brock point out, these evaluations must be proportional to the *potential losses* for each player. For example, patients are correctly held to a higher standard of competence when refusing life-sustaining treatment compared to when they are buying cigarettes or plane tickets. Both outcomes produce some increased health risk, but the risk in plane travel is almost negligible, while the risk in foregoing treatment for late-stage cancer is maximal. Translating this idea into the language of our ethics engine: higher potential losses will require a higher standard for informed and voluntary consensual override. For instance, in countries like the Netherlands that have legalized physician-assisted suicide, this practice comes along with rigorous conditions for patient competence. Patients requesting life-ending treatments must be assessed by two psychiatrists and have a waiting period of six months or more to consider their decision. A maximal loss of health should be accompanied by a maximal standard for consent. Factors like age of the patient, cognitive abilities, intoxication levels, psychiatric evaluation, active threats from other humans, and how much time available to act are all relevant ways to evaluate whether a patient is making an informed and voluntary choice. The standards for consensual updating should proportionally go up when the potential losses go up.

Let's apply this consent procedure to another example: robotic tattoo artists. Tattoos often involve a significant change in personal appearance, which brings some risk of losing psychological self-esteem. Very large and visible tattoos (say, a spider tattoo that takes up somebody's entire face) would come along with a high standard of consent. But how would a robotic tattoo artist confirm this high standard? Measurements like cognitive tests and blood testing might ensure that a person is not intoxicated and understands the relevant consequences. A waiting period and required online course completion could ensure that the client understands the statistics on how often people get tattoos removed and hear about other people's experiences with them. After sufficiently demonstrating that this choice is voluntary and well informed, it should be acceptable for a robot to give the client a full-face spider tattoo. (If there's any sentence in the book that's ripe for being taken out of context, it's that one.)

The Leximin procedure

Maximin roughly states: "Pick the action with the highest minimum value." For data sets without any ties, this procedure is relatively simple. Consider a simple case of two actions and four players, shown in Figure 5.4.

Although the first action has a higher sum of payoffs, Maximin will pick the second, because its minimum value is higher (the minimum values are highlighted). This result can be generated by two basic procedures, call them MIN and MAX;

MIN: Find the lowest payoff in each action
MAX: Assemble these minimums together, and pick the highest of the minimums

We could use a simple linear search algorithm for both procedures. A linear search algorithm will start from the beginning of each action profile and crank

		P1	P2	P3	P4
	A1	5	**2**	9	8
✓	A2	4	6	5	**3**

FIGURE 5.4 A simple data set: two action profiles for four players. Minimum values are bolded. Even though A1 has a higher sum of payoffs, Maximin selects A2.

through the series, item by item.[5] MIN and MAX are good enough for simple action profiles without any tied values. However, for action profiles with ties, we'll need to add a bit more.

The simplest case of a tie would be two actions with a single equal minimum value, like (3, 5) and (3, 6). Even though the "worst" outcome in both these cases is equal, it's obvious that a rational agent from the original position would simply delete or cover these tied minimum values and move on to the "next-worst" values. Assuming an equal chance of being the next player as well, we would be equally interested in maximizing her minimum. This gives a clear procedure for evaluating ties: cover up the tied values and move on to the next-lowest values. Call this procedure NEXTBEST.[6] But there are two parts of NEXTBEST that need to be further specified.

The easy part is what to do if you've covered up all the ties, and there aren't any more values in either profile? This will only occur when each payoff in one action profile has a one-to-one correspondence with an outcome in the other profile (in other words, one set of payoffs is just a permutation of the other), like: (8, 6, 3) and (3, 8, 6). The solution to this problem seems clear if we are using standard decision theory from the original position. When the arrangement of goods is exactly equal in two possible actions, a rational agent will randomize. In distributions that have a one-to-one correspondence, we simply flip a coin to decide between them.[7]

The difficult issue with NEXTBEST is what to do when there are multiple ties for minimum values. Do we cover up *all* the tied values, or just the *first* tied value we find in each profile? Consider the action profiles: A1 = (3, −8, −8) and A2 = (−8, 2, 8). The minimum values for A1 and A2 are the same, but there are two instances of the minimum value in A1, and only one instance of it in A2. What do we do? Cover up *all* the tied values, or just the first one (Figure 5.5)? Let's give names to each of these options. In a paper I wrote in 2016, I argued that Rawls would have advocated covering all the tied values, and I called this procedure *Maximin+*.

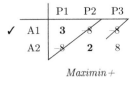

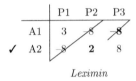

FIGURE 5.5 Two potential methods for resolving the tie produced by (3, −8, −8) and (−8, 2, 8). The Maximin+ approach covers all ties, and produces A1 as the winner. The Leximin approach only covers the first instance of tied values, producing A2 as the winner.

There are also several papers from computational game theory which discuss the Maximin principle combined with covering just the single tied value (apparently without any recognition that this connects with Rawls or Contractarianism), and they have called this procedure *Leximin*. In Figure 5.5, we see that Maximin+ will pick A1, while Leximin will pick A2.

Should we use Maximin+ or Leximin? This isn't a minor problem; it's essential to producing a solution to trolley-style dilemmas. In a standard version of the trolley dilemma, we could significantly lower the survival of one person to raise the survival of many others, or vice versa. Using the same table of payoffs from Chapter 1, these two options would produce very different results. Maximin+ covers all the tied values, in which case we should randomize. On the other hand, Leximin covers just a single tied minimum value, so it produces the standard utilitarian solution: prefer the suffering of a few to the suffering of many, when this suffering is of equal value (Figure 5.6).

The previous chapter argued that Rawls would advocate a "thick" version of the original position, and I still endorse the claim from my 2016 paper that Rawls would endorse the Maximin+ principle. However, as I've come to realize, the Maximin+ principle does not always produce Pareto-optimal solutions to cooperation problems, while the Leximin principle does (see this footnote for a formal proof).[8] I failed to see this when I originally endorsed the Maximin+ principle, mostly because I had been focusing my attention on distributions between only two players rather than those involving more than two. Once we expand our scope to interactions involving n-number of players, this procedure simply fails the Pareto-optimality standard for a successful moral theory. For example, in a simple choice between a distribution of (1, 2, 2) and (1, 1, 2), covering up all the tied minimums will lead us to be indifferent between these outcomes. But the first distribution is clearly a Pareto-improvement on the second. On the other hand, if we cover up only the first instance of a tied value, then this procedure will always produce both Pareto-optimality and cooperative behavior. Therefore, the Leximin principle is the approach we should use to settle ties in minimum values.[9]

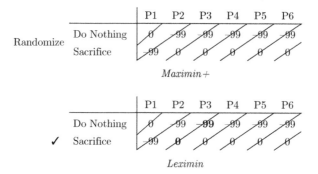

FIGURE 5.6 Two potential methods for resolving the trolley problem, using the methods from Figure 5.5. Covering all ties will randomize, while covering a single tie will select the sacrifice option.

90 Ethics engines

Putting this together, the combination of MIN, MAX, and NEXTBEST into the Leximin procedure looks like the following:

> Do a linear search to find the lowest values in each action profile, and put these in a set. Do another linear search on this set to find the highest value, and discard all the losing actions.
> If there's only one action left, it's the winner.
> If there is more than one action remaining, delete the first element in the remaining profiles equal to the tied minimum value, then run MIN and MAX again.
> Keep doing this until there's a unique winner.
> If there are no more values in either action to delete, randomize between them.[10]

For the visual learners, I've represented the procedure as a flowchart (Figure 5.7).

The flowchart is designed with typicality in mind. The three different columns (not including the input and output) are ordered from the most typical to the least typical paths. By far the most typical paths will trace a straight line down the first column and reach a single decision. Less typically, there will be

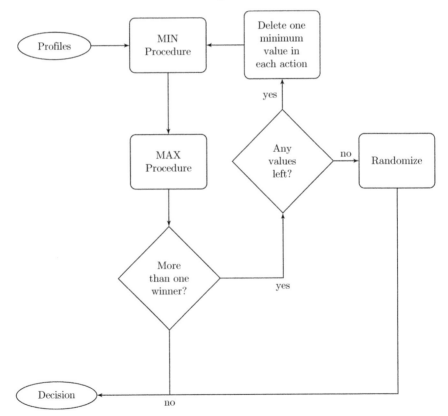

FIGURE 5.7 The Leximin procedure as a flowchart.

ties for the Maximin value, and the path will proceed up through the second column and back down through the first again. In even more rare cases, this will continue in a circular path until a unique value is reached. Finally, in the rarest of circumstances, a one-to-one correspondence between action profiles, the path will proceed to the third column and randomize.

The Leximin procedure is extremely powerful, and can be extended to a wide variety of decision spaces. I'll finish the discussion here by showing how we could apply the algorithm to a decision-tree with multiple layers, like we might see in a chess engine. In chess, the strategy algorithm typically proceeds level-by-level, starting at the bottom (the outcomes furthest in the future) and working backwards. The idea is to identify the best future end-state and work towards it. If these values are measurements of chess pieces and position, all that matters is the final outcome of the game. But if the values are measurements of people's primary goods like health and opportunity, a chess strategy is unacceptable. According to Contractarianism, there are magnitudes of harm and restricted opportunity that are unacceptable to inflict on people, even if it winds up producing greater overall benefits for them in the long run. Because of that, when we apply Leximin to a decision-tree, we should group together the payoffs in each of the child nodes of a branch. Consider the decision trees in Figure 5.8.

In the first tree, there are only two options, A1 and A2. Using the Leximin procedure we've defined, it's easy to determine that A2 is the better choice. To make this even more clear, I've denoted the minimum values for each action profile on the edges of each branch. But now let's imagine that the robot is capable of looking ahead to the choices it can make from A1 and A2, which are A3–A6, represented at the bottom nodes of the second decision-tree. Now it looks like the right-branching path leads to undesirable Leximin results. Finally, in the last tree, the choices that branch from these outcomes produce mixed results: A12 creates the highest Maximin value, but to get there, we have to go through the lowest Maximin value at node A5. A utilitarian might say, "It all works out in the end," but Contractarianism would reject exposing the worst-off person to terrible harms and restrictions, even if it will all be more beneficial to her in the long run. This is because a distribution of goods spread out in time is not different from a distribution of goods spread through space. In concrete terms, this means calculating the Leximin procedure over *paths* of actions rather than individual time-slice outcomes.

In the decision-tree depicted at the bottom of Figure 5.8, there are 13 states (A1–A13), but only six potential paths through these states:

Path 1: A1 > A3 > A7
Path 2: A1 > A3 > A8
Path 3: A1 > A4 > A8
Path 4: A2 > A5 > A11
Path 5: A2 > A5 > A12
Path 6: A2 > A6 > A8

92 Ethics engines

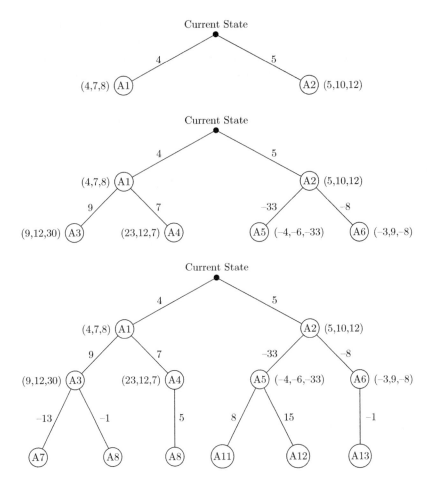

FIGURE 5.8 Three levels of a decision-tree, where the numbers at each action (node) represent payoffs of primary goods for three players, and the numbers at each branch (edge) represent the minimum value of the action below them. I've omitted payoffs for the third level at the bottom. Although we haven't discussed incorporating likelihoods, these could be included as a coefficient of the payoffs at each node (as in standard decision-theoretic trees).

Using the minimum values associated with each state (represented on the branches), we can turn these paths into temporal path profiles, much like an action profile:

Path 1: A1 > A3 > A7 = (4, 9, −13)
Path 2: A1 > A3 > A8 = (4, 9, −1)
Path 3: A1 > A4 > A8 = (4, 7, 5)
Path 4: A2 > A5 > A11 = (5, −33, 8)
Path 5: A2 > A5 > A12 = (5, −33, 15)
Path 6: A2 > A6 > A8 = (5, −8, −1)

Now we can run the usual Leximin procedure over these path profiles. The winner is Path 2, with the highest minimum value of 4. Notice that the end-result of this path is an outcome with a lower minimum value than some of the other end-result nodes (like A11 and A12). This is not the move that a chess player would take, but when playing chess with real people's health and opportunity, it's the move that a Contractarian would make.

Chapter summary

- Using chess engines as a model, we can design an abstract "ethics engine" that incorporates a Contractarian moral theory. Such an ethics engine would involve four components: (1) the current state of all self-interested players and their distributions of primary goods, (2) a map of all the available actions and their likely outcomes of primary good states, (3) an evaluation of the difference between each player's current state of primary goods and their predicted payoffs of primary goods, (3.5) an option to update the distribution of primary goods based on players' reported preferences, and (4) a modified version of the Maximin principle, called Leximin.
- The players parameter should only have access to information about features that are relevant to the distribution of primary goods. This means omitting information about social-relational facts like a person's occupation, race, religion, sexual orientation, or anything else that will (by definition) produce discrimination in making moral choices.
- Quantifying states of primary goods like health, opportunity, and essential resources is very difficult, but it is possible to make more or less accurate estimates of these states.
- Since primary goods are a default measurement of what an individual player prefers, they should be sensitive to updating these values based on explicit corrections from the players themselves. This is the role of consent.
- The original Maximin principle does not always produce unique outcomes in cases where there are tied minimum values. There are two ways of modifying the rule: Maximin+ and Leximin. Although I believe that Rawls would advocate Maximin+ (as I did in a previous publication), it is provable that Leximin will produce Pareto-optimal results in cases where Maximin+ fails, and so it is the superior rule.
- The Leximin rule can be applied to large decision trees by turning each path into its own action-profile.

Notes

1 It's theoretically possible to map out every possible chess game by completing this tree with every board position from every move. If a machine could do this, it could always force a win or a draw (this is sometimes called *solving chess*). The problem

94 Ethics engines

is that there are an astounding number of possible outcomes. In 1950, Claude Shannon observed this:

> In typical chess positions there will be on the order of 30 legal moves ... A typical game lasts about 40 moves to resignation of one party ... even at this figure there will be 10^{120} [possible chess games, derived from 30 to the power of 80 (40 moves for each player)]

In other words, there are more nodes in the complete tree of chess than particles in the known universe! Representing this much data is obviously impractical, so chess programs today will look only a few moves down the road, where the number of states they represent is on the order of millions or tens of millions.

2   The evaluation function would then sum the differences between these weighed values (where Q is my queen and Q' is my opponent's queen):

$$9(Q-Q')+5(R-R')+3(B-B')+3(K-K')+(P-P')$$

For example, if you lost your queen and I lost two of my rooks, the function would output: $9(1) + 5(-2) + 3(0) + 3(0) + (0) = -1$. This means I'm losing.

3   An early example of this comes from Peter Danielson's *Artificial Morality* (1992), where he created computer programs that interacted with each other in cooperation games over long periods of time. Rather than a homogenous group of cooperators who always maximized the minimum value, the result was something that looked very much like human history: tribes of cooperators separating from tribes of defectors, wars between the tribes, the emergence of occasional criminals within cooperative groups, and so on.

4   One problem is that it fails to distinguish between opportunities lost due to blindness itself and opportunities lost due to discrimination against the blind.

5   A linear search algorithm for Procedure MIN (Data) would look like this:

```
Procedure MIN(Data):
    For each A_i in data:
        Initialize min_i to A_i[0]
        For each value in A_i
            If this value is smaller than min_i
                Replace min_i with this value
        Return min_i for all i
```

The MAX procedure takes the MinVals as input, so we'll write: Procedure MAX (MinVals). The procedure can be written as the following linear search algorithm:

```
Procedure MAX(MinVals):
    Initialize max to 0
    For each Min_i
        If Min_i is larger than max
            Replace max with Min_i
    Return Min_i with (each value < max) replaced with -1
```

6   Procedure NextBest(Data, MaxVals):
   For each A$_i$ in Data with MaxVals$_i$ = [sentinel value], remove A$_i$ from Data
   For each A$_i$ in Data with MaxVals$_i$ > [sentinel value]:
       Remove the first occurrence of MaxVals$_i$ from A$_i$
   Set MinVals$_i$ to output of MIN(Data)
   Set MaxVals$_i$ to output of MAX(MinVals$_i$)
   Return MaxVals

7   The randomization can be added to NEXTBEST:

   If A$_i$ is empty:
       Choose at random one MaxVals$_i$ not equal to [sentinel value],
       and replace all others with [sentinel value] Return MaxVals

8   Assume there are two distributions of payoffs, A and B, where A is a Pareto-improvement on B. Then, by definition:

   Each element of A, A1–An, corresponds with some element in B1–Bn, and vice versa (this is just to say that Player 1's payoff in A is A1, and Player 1's payoff in B is B1).

   Every element, A1–An, is greater or equal to its corresponding element, B1–Bn.

   There is at least one element of A that is greater than its corresponding element in B.

   Let A and B be ordered from their lowest-valued elements to their highest-valued elements. Leximin begins with the lowest elements of each distribution, A1 and B1. Because A is a Pareto-improvement on B, either A1>B1, or A1=B1. If A1>B1, then Leximin produces A. If A1=B1, then Leximin proceeds to A2 and B2.
   Because A is a Pareto-improvement on B, either A2>B2, or A2=B2. If A2>B2, then Leximin produces A. If A2=B2, then Leximin proceeds to A3 and B3.
   This process will continue until it reaches some element in A that is greater than its corresponding element in B, and will then produce A. Because at least one of these elements exists, Leximin will produce A.

9   This is what I called in Chapter 3 a "theory-external" argument, but there is also a "theory-internal" argument for only covering the first instance of a tied value. Roughly: if you could easily wind up being anybody, it *matters* whether you could wind up being two people who are better off versus just one. This isn't the same as calculating the probability of being one of the people, as with Harsanyi's expected value rule, which allows us to outweigh the suffering of one person with the happiness of many people. Instead, this rule says that the *equal* suffering of many people is objectively worse than the equal suffering of a single person, no matter what person you might wind up being. A similar argument has been made by the Contractarian philosopher Thomas Scanlon (1998), who suggests that the person whose outcomes are just lumped in with the outcomes of other people has a real claim to make that

her life is being unfairly discounted. Just as the expected value rule unfairly allows one person's outcomes to be distorted, Scanlon argues that the Maximin+ rule allows one person's outcomes to be homogenized or ignored. This is basically correct. It also brings in a lot of what is intuitive about utilitarianism: numbers *do* matter, but only when the changes to primary goods are of equal values. The number of people who benefit or suffer matters, but individual agreement still matters more. Using Leximin finds a place for the importance of numbers in Contractarianism in an organic way that follows straightforwardly from the original position.

10 Procedure LEXIMIN(Data):

Set MinVals$_i$ to output of MIN(Data)

Set MaxVals$_i$ to output of MAX(MinVals$_i$)

If exactly one maxVals$_i$ > -1, then return the A$_i$ corresponding to that maxVals$_i$

While there are more than one MaxVals_i > -1:

Set MaxVals to output of NEXTBEST(Data, MaxVals)

References

Buchannan, Allen & Brock, Dan (1989). *Deciding for Others: The Ethics of Surrogate Decision-making.* Cambridge: Cambridge University Press.

Danielson, Peter (1992). *Artificial Morality: Virtuous Robots for Virtual Games.* New York: Routledge.

Scanlon, Thomas (1998). *What We Owe to Each Other.* Cambridge, MA: Belknap Press.

6

AVOIDING COLLISIONS

On October 5, 2008, Katerina Wyakimovich was driving through a sudden burst of rain on a street in Clearwater, Florida. Around the same time, a 72-year-old man was taking refuge from the rain within a bus shelter down the road. As reported by the *Tampa Bay Times*, the car that Wyakimovich was driving suddenly encountered a large pool of standing water and began to hydroplane. The car careened into the shelter, killing the man who was waiting out the storm. There were no implications that Wyakimovich was speeding or intoxicated.

According to the U.S. Federal Highway Administration, 7,400 people are killed in weather-related vehicle crashes each year, and 75 percent of these involve wet pavement. Hydroplaning and slipping can be prevented by taking steps like taking your foot off the accelerator, avoiding sudden movements, and turning into the direction the car is sliding. Unfortunately, human drivers are very bad at these kinds of responses during emergency situations. We tend to flail around, speed up, and turn away. On the other hand, if computers take control of cars in these situations, they will inevitably be more capable of making the right movements. This is just one way that autonomous vehicles may be a way of preventing thousands of fatalities every year.

If there had been a computer in control of Katerina Wyakimovich's car in 2008, could it have avoided the tragedy? It depends on a lot of factors, like how much time was available, and how much traction the brakes still had. Hydroplaning occurs when there is too much water building up between tires and the road. It's possible that a car driven by a computer might not be able to regain control of the brakes, but still maintain some control of steering. If there were enough time available, the computer would have been able to swerve away from its deadly path. Generally, it's a bad idea to swerve in hydroplaning situations; the car might crash into other obstacles or flip over. But in this situation, the risks to Ms. Wyakimovich would have been lower than the risks to the elderly man in the shelter, given that the car had airbags and she was wearing a seatbelt. Of course, the computer can only make a decision like this if it's already programmed to do so. This means that we, the designers, now have to address the question: should a computer be programmed to swerve in order to avoid hitting a pedestrian, despite some significant increase in risk to the driver?

Situations like these are rare, but they have captured public interest. Between 2015 and 2016, there were dozens of articles written about this dilemma, with headlines like:

> Should Your Driverless Car Hit a Pedestrian to Save Your Life?
> (New York Times, *June 23, 2016*)

> The Self-Driving Dilemma: Should Your Car Kill You to Save Others?
> (Popular Mechanics, *June 23, 2016*)

> Your Driverless Car Could Be Programmed to Kill You.
> (New York Magazine, *October 28, 2015*)

In 2016, two representatives of Mercedes-Benz publicly remarked that their driverless vehicles would always protect the car's passengers in a collision situation. According to *Car and Driver Magazine*, the company's manager of driver-assist systems and active safety, Christoph Von Hugo, made the following comment at an auto show in Paris:

> If you know you can save at least one person, at least save that one. Save the one in the car ... If all you know for sure is that one death can be prevented, then that's your first priority.

Separately, in an interview with *The Australian*, the company's Australia spokesman David McCarthy agreed:

> If there is someone literally jumping in front of you, in that circumstance, there's nothing technology can do except reduce speed of impact ... I would say that the vehicle is designed inside to protect the people inside.

Just a few days later, the *Daily Mail* featured this headline:

> Mercedes-Benz admits automated driverless cars would run over a CHILD rather than swerve and risk injuring the passengers inside.
> (*October 14, 2016*)

This headline is obviously an overreaction to the remarks we read, but as car companies have learned, there's really no way of talking about this issue without producing an overreaction. If the representatives had said that the car should swerve and protect pedestrians, the headline would have been "Your Driverless

Car Could Be Programmed to Kill You." The point is that there's no way of evaluating collisions without some terrible-sounding headline, which is probably why most manufacturers have tried to avoid commenting on it. In that same story from *Car and Driver* that got negative headlines, Christoph Von Hugo insisted that this moral dilemma isn't as pressing as we might think:

> This moral question of whom to save: 99 percent of our engineering work is to prevent these situations from happening at all. We are working so our cars don't drive into situations where that could happen and [will] drive away from potential situations where those decisions have to be made.

This is the most common response that I get from engineers that I've spoken to: ethics algorithms aren't even necessary, since the technology will prevent situations like the trolley problem from ever presenting themselves in the first place. Admittedly, the engineers have a point here. Most of the scenarios imagined by philosophers and the popular press involve the vehicle's brakes failing or some unseen object popping into the vehicle's path. But these situations are extremely unlikely given the large number of redundant emergency systems that reduce the problem of machine failure, and improvements in perceptual range that make "unseen objects a negligible concern. The real problems won't come from brake failures or unseen objects, but unexpected behavior. Until driverless vehicles have provably perfect safety, it's necessary to specify ways of evaluating which collisions are better and worse than others.

In a 2016 article for *The Guardian*, reporters asked engineers at Google's driverless vehicle company for their responses to trolley-style moral dilemmas. The principal engineer on the project, Andrew Chatham, replied that they'd never encountered a moral dilemma situation "in all our journeys." Google is very proud of the fact that its driverless cars have logged over 1.4 million miles, with only one minor collision. Yet drivers in the United States alone logged about 3 trillion (with a *t*) miles in 2014. With around 30,000 fatal car crashes, that's a rate of one fatal car crash per 100 million miles. Google would need to run its driverless cars another *99 million miles* without a single fatal car crash just to demonstrate the same level of safety as humans currently have.

I don't mean to express skepticism about the safety of driverless cars. On the contrary, I am cautiously optimistic that they will eventually surpass human performance by leaps and bounds. In their book, *Driverless* (2016), Hod Lipson and Melba Kurman suggest that driverless cars should be at least two or three times safer than human-driven cars before they are widely available. But even if driverless cars are *ten* times safer than human-driven cars, they will still have a fatal car crash once every billion miles. This brings the death toll down significantly, but still produces roughly 3,000 fatal crashes annually. Given that we're talking about the lives of thousands of people every year just in the U.S. alone, this conversation can't be ignored.

Even if actual moral dilemmas are never encountered by driverless vehicles, it's useful to think about extreme cases that occur *downstream* from more everyday decisions. In bioethics, students are asked to consider extreme and unusual situations, such as a patient refusing a harmless treatment that's needed to save her life, for no apparent reason. The purpose of encouraging medical students to think hard about these cases is that it helps them adjust their attitudes and behaviors upstream from this situation, like how aggressive and respectful to treat patients in small-scale everyday interactions. In the case of driverless vehicles, thinking about extreme cases will help us to design algorithms for making minor changes in where the vehicle angles itself as it slows down or stops to avoid dangers. Just like the small-scale behaviors of doctors, these actions can add up to important consequences over millions of interactions.

Finally, even if driverless cars accomplish perfect safety, so long as a system is working to avoid collisions, it's always evaluating which ones are better and worse, and so it's implicitly making moral judgments. A navigation system that treats a collision with every obstacle as equally bad is implicitly assuming no difference between humans and objects. Most engineers aren't thinking about these assumptions, because they would prefer not to have to dwell on hard moral problems, just like all of us. Unfortunately, there's no way of avoiding ethics when navigating through an uncertain world filled with people.

A crash course in driverless vehicles (or, "Highway to the danger cone")

The first tournament for driverless vehicles, sponsored by the U.S. Department of Defense, took place in 2004. The setting was a 150-mile course through the Mojave Desert. Fifteen teams from companies and universities entered their vehicles in a race to complete the course. The winner would receive a million dollar prize. That first year, none of the teams finished the race. The next year would see five teams reach the finish line, with the winning vehicle (Stanford's *Stanley*) receiving the now-doubled $2 million prize. These tournaments are widely recognized as the beginning of viable autonomous vehicles, and within ten years, companies like Google and Uber had logged hundreds of thousands of miles on their driverless cars through urban centers like San Francisco and Pittsburgh.

In 2016, the Society of Automotive Engineers released a classification system for driving technologies that can easily apply to any domain of robots:

> Level 0: An automatic system that issues warnings but has no control over actions
> Level 1: A human and robot are in collaborative control of actions ("hands on")
> Level 2: A robot is in full control of actions, but a human must be supervising at all times ("hands off")
> Level 3: A robot is in full control of actions, but a human must be prepared to intervene periodically ("eyes off")
> Level 4: A robot is in full unsupervised control in certain conditions
> Level 5: A robot is in full unsupervised control in all conditions.

The vehicles that we're most interested in are fully autonomous ones (Levels 4–5), although an ethics engine could also be relevant at the more semi-autonomous stages as well (Levels 2–3).

A driverless vehicle system will need to have components like a human mind: faculties of perception, memory, planning, and motion execution. Just like a human walking around a city, the vehicle will need to represent the world and categorize objects, remember how they usually move and interact, plan a good route that maximizes its goals, and turn this plan into actual movements.

Within the perceptual system, a vehicle will collect data from LIDAR, RADAR, GPS, and camera sensors to create a large and impressive map of its surroundings. It will also need a way to make *sense* of this information, categorizing objects as bicycles, pedestrians, vehicles, and other kinds of objects, while at the same time predicting how each of these objects usually behaves. In his popular TED talk, *How a Driverless Car Sees the Road*, Google's Chris Urmson describes the results of these high-powered imaging technologies and object recognition systems:

> [The driverless vehicle] starts by understanding where it is in the world, by taking a map and its sensor data and aligning the two, and then we layer on top of that what it sees in the moment. So here, all the purple boxes you can see are other vehicles on the road, and the red thing on the side over there is a cyclist, and up in the distance, if you look really closely, you can see some cones. Then we know where the car is in the moment, but we have to do better than that: we have to predict what's going to happen. So here the pickup truck in top right is about to make a left lane change because the road in front of it is closed, so it needs to get out of the way.

Urmson explains that the vehicle's computer identifies objects as pedestrians or bicyclists and then predicts what it expects them to do based on their current positions and movements (Figure 6.1).

Predicting the behavior of other objects is an incredibly difficult task. Google recently filed a patent titled: "Modifying Behavior of Driverless Vehicle Based on Predicted Behavior of Other Vehicles" (US Patent #US9330571, 2016). It's boring to read, but luckily, it's filled with exciting ideas. Here is an excerpt:

> The method also includes determining … a predicted behavior of the at least one other vehicle based on at least the current state of the vehicle and the current state of the environment of the vehicle. The method further includes determining, using the computer system, a confidence level. The confidence level includes a likelihood of the at least one other vehicle to perform the predicted behavior.

This "confidence level" is crucial; it's a way of attaching a margin of error to every predicted path. At the point where the vehicle is right now, there's a very

FIGURE 6.1   The perceptual systems of an autonomous vehicle will take information from LIDAR, RADAR, GPS, and camera sensors, and integrate it with a set of categories of objects like "vehicle" and "pedestrian," along with expectations and predictions of how these objects move. Image from Chris Urmson's TED talk: "How a Driverless Car Sees the Road."

low margin of error. But as the predicted path gets further from the vehicle's current state, the confidence level gets lower. As Lipson and Kurman (2016) describe, this is just like the way that meteorologists depict the path of a hurricane as an expanding cone: the area of the cone represents all the possible places that the hurricane might travel based on its current position and velocity, and our best understanding of typical hurricane patterns. The larger the area of the cone, the greater the uncertainty. Thus, the title *cone of uncertainty*. Moving vehicles will have larger cones of uncertainty compared to pedestrians, and vehicles at higher speeds will have larger cones than ones at lower speeds.[1]

In this model, what does it mean to predict that a collision is likely? I'll assume it means that the predicted paths of two objects collide, with the paths having relatively high confidence levels (that is, small cones of uncertainty). Humans are good at this; if you're watching a car rapidly approaching another car in its lane, there's a point where you start to get worried that it's not slowing down fast enough. As the car gets closer, alarm bells start going off in your mind, and you say to yourself: "Holy shit, that SUV is going to hit the car in front of it!" A group of researchers led by Thierry Fraichard (2004) have spent several years establishing the exact mathematical details of the point at which predicted paths will certainly collide, which they call *inevitable collision states*. Somewhere between an inevitable collision state and a normal predicted path is a point at which the predicted paths of two objects cross a threshold that is dangerously close, where a reasonable driver might begin to shout: "Holy shit!" Let's call this range the *danger cone*. Exactly what the threshold is for the danger cone doesn't really matter for our purposes; it's some subsection of the cone of uncertainty between normal safe driving and inevitable collision states.

We want the vehicle to plan its route to avoid other objects and their danger cones. Once the vehicle strays inside the danger cone of another vehicle, a collision becomes likely. A safe computer will make sure to drive slower around larger cones than small ones. Thinking in terms of danger cones can help us to define a moral dilemma situation:

> A moral dilemma for driverless vehicles occurs whenever *every* possible action leads its predicted path into the danger cone of another object.

How frequently will vehicles encounter situations like this, and how frequently do vehicles currently encounter them? It's difficult to have any data about this, but we can certainly model dilemma scenarios and develop programs that deal with them in a morally acceptable way.

This is the point at which planning and control systems enter the picture. There are many different methods for robotic path planning, and several excellent textbooks on the subject (Choset et al., 2005). I won't pretend to give an overview of them here, and I wouldn't be qualified to do so anyway. Instead, I'll give a general description of a family of approaches to planning and control. Assume the vehicle's perceptual system has produced a map of the environment, classifications for each object in the environment, and predicted paths for each object along with some measure of confidence. Call this a *model*. The vehicle also has a goal, and routes the most efficient paths to reach that goal within its current model. But some of these paths will venture into the danger cones of other objects, so these paths are either pruned away or ranked lower than collision-free paths. The control system will then take steps to follow the best path in a smooth and efficient way. As the vehicle moves, it will frequently update its model, which leads to a new set of preferred paths, and more adjustments to behavior from the control system.

Consider a case study in this kind of planning system: an autonomous wheelchair developed by Benjamin Kuipers and Jong Jin Park (2014). This wheelchair is fully functional and capable of navigating throughout the busy hallways of the University of Michigan without colliding with objects or people. The wheelchair plans and updates its route based on an approach called *model predictive control*. It uses sensors to build a map of the terrain, representing all the stationary and moving objects within the environment, as well as making some prediction of where they're going to move next. The navigation system casts around 400 possible paths from its current position, then detects which ones are likely to result in collisions, based on the predicted paths of objects in the environment (Figure 6.2).

A standard convention in path-planning is to indicate the collision paths in red and the collision-free paths in green.[2] As you might imagine, when a vehicle or wheelchair is in an open space, most of these paths will be green, and when it is surrounded by many objects or predicted objects, most of the paths will be red (Figure 6.3).

Avoiding collisions

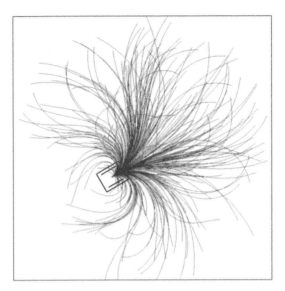

FIGURE 6.2 An example of 300 randomly selected paths from the set of smooth and physically possible paths. Image from Jong Jin Park's dissertation: "Graceful Navigation for Mobile Robots in Dynamic and Uncertain Environments."

(a) (b)

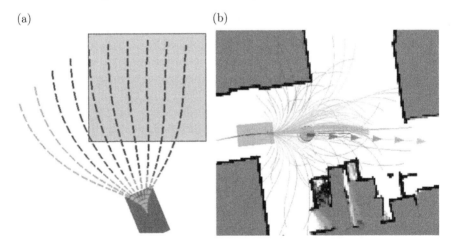

FIGURE 6.3 (a) The likelihood of collision is here indicated by the amount of red on a path. (b) The system predicts the movements of a pedestrian (indicated by the triangles) and which paths produce more likely collisions. Image from Jong-Jin Park's dissertation: "Graceful Navigation for Mobile Robots in Dynamic and Uncertain Environments."

The wheelchair then integrates this map of collision-free paths with its map of the most efficient paths to reach its goal, and updates its movements from the original route to this new route. One of the most amazing things is that the system is updating its path up to five times per second. This approach is only one way of navigating through a dynamically changing environment, but at a broad level, any driverless vehicle will be using something that looks like it: planning an efficient route to the goal, predicting the paths of other objects, creating a map of better and worse paths based on collisions, updating the route based on this field. The part where our ethics engine becomes relevant is evaluating paths based on collision states.

Evaluating collisions

As engineers point out, all the paths resulting in collisions are bad. But as philosophers point out, some of them are worse than others. Even in a world where vehicles can avoid collisions entirely, they will still need to evaluate which ones are worse in the process of slowing down or veering away from more dangerous situations. How do we design a vehicle to evaluate collisions? The first obvious way to measure this is by likelihood: likely collisions are generally worse than unlikely collisions. Likelihood is very important, but it's not the only thing that matters. Consider whether you would prefer a high probability of being hit by a paper plane or a medium probability of being hit by an actual airplane. What we need to consider is both the likelihood *and* the damage done in each collision. The only way to make sense of "damage" in a moral sense, according to Contractarianism, is the loss of primary goods. I'll assume that the key primary good that's lost in car crashes is health, so this will be our measurement of how severe a collision is. Even more, I'll use probability of survival or death as a proxy for general health, where healthier people have a greater probability of survival, and less healthy people have a greater probability of death. Basically, I'm proposing a single-dimensional scale of severe injury, with death being the most extreme point on this scale.[3] I'm willing to revise this, and perhaps consider the most extreme kind of injury to be the most debilitating and painful injury that one could still survive. However, it seems easier to use databases of fatalities and injuries that are more or less likely to lead to fatality, since there are massive databases of information about collision fatalities in existence, as well as information about the velocities and angles of impact that led to these fatalities.

Let's assume that our autonomous vehicle is tracking the relative velocity and angle of orientation with respect to the vehicle at all times. For every object in the environment, our computer should ask: how fast is this object moving relative to me, in what direction is it moving, and what is its angle of orientation? A vehicle moving straight towards me at 30mph when I am moving at 20mph has a relative velocity of 50mph with respect to me, and since it's pointed directly at me, the angle relative to my orientation is 0. In addition, each obstacle will be categorized as a physical object, a pedestrian, a cyclist, or a vehicle, and assigned a value for its estimated occupancy. Categorizing the type of an object is important for determining how much protection each person has in a collision, where pedestrians have less protection than vehicle passengers. The size of the vehicle is relevant, and even for pedestrians and

106 Avoiding collisions

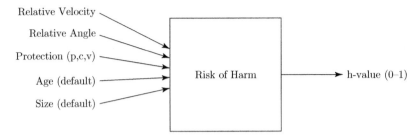

FIGURE 6.4 Risk of harm as a function of the relative velocity and angle between two objects, how much protection the person has (categorized as pedestrian, cyclist, or vehicle), and the age and size of the person. The output of this function will be a real number between 0 and 1, interpreted as the "risk of harm" (h-value) to a particular person with respect to the robot. Factors like the distance between two objects, likelihood of collision, and how many people are in the vehicle are omitted here but still part of the calculation.

passengers themselves, it would also be useful to have physical information like their size and age. If it's impossible to collect this data, these values can be set to a default value based on average age and size (same with vehicle occupancy). This information will all be input into a function that determines the risk of harm for every player, formalized as a real-numbered value between 0 and 1 that can be called an *h-value* (Figure 6.4). The justification for this is intuitively clear: a person faces a greater risk of fatal harm when an object is moving faster towards her, at a closer angle of orientation, and she has less protection from it.

This is meant to be a calculation for every individual player; vehicles with an estimated occupancy of three people will get three separate h-values for risk of harm. The estimation of distance and likelihood of collision is a separate calculation that will be integrated with this one.

For example, imagine you are a single passenger within an autonomous vehicle. There are five objects in our field of vision: a wall, a pedestrian, a cyclist, and two vehicles. The h-value for collision-free paths will be set to 0. The h-value for paths that collide with the wall will be a single value, representing the estimated harm to you in that collision. There will be two h-values for paths colliding with the pedestrian: one for you and one for the pedestrian. Same for paths that collide with the cyclist. How many h-values are assigned to the vehicle collision paths? It depends on the estimated occupancy of the vehicles. If a vehicle has three people, there will be four h-values: three for their vehicle and one for ours.

Nothing that's been described so far has involved moral assumptions, but it's impossible to proceed any further without making some major ones. It would be nice if we could just program an autonomous vehicle to "avoid the worst harms," but there's no self-evident way to determine which are the *worst*. We have an h-value for each player along each path, but these values need to be integrated into a single number to say which path is the worst. In the path that collides with the cyclist, let's say the h-value is 10 for the agent vehicle and 80 for the cyclist.

Do we add these together, making that path have a risk of 90? Do we pick the worst-off player, the cyclist, and use her payoff to give the path a risk of 80? Or do we pick the passenger in the driverless vehicle and give the path a risk of 10? One of these uses a utilitarian principle, the other uses a Contractarian principle, and the third uses a principle of pure self-interest:

> Utilitarian principle: Sum the harm risks in collision-paths
> Contractarian principle: Use the highest harm risk in collision-paths
> Self-interest principle: Use the agent's harm risk in collision-paths

Just like moral theories, each of these principles will produce very safe motion in normal situations. Most of the situations that philosophers and journalists have created to compare these principles are not precise enough to produce different responses. A utilitarian vehicle will steer towards free space and come to a complete stop to avoid most collisions, just like a Contractarian vehicle. But one of them might swerve slightly towards the cyclist, and the other might swerve slightly towards another vehicle. Over millions and millions of interactions, these slight differences can add up to produce real differences in the amount and type of collisions that occur. The best way to test these principles against each other would be to implement them into a simulation with millions of interactions over long periods of time, and adjust the speeds and number of objects across conditions. I predict that a utilitarian algorithm will produce fewer total collisions, while the Contractarian algorithm might produce fewer *fatal* collisions, and reduce the worst kind of damage in collisions overall.

A potential field implementation

A terrain of morally better or worse outcomes is what Sam Harris (2011) calls a "moral landscape," where the best options might be blocked by some very bad ones. In these scenarios, we might be more interested in navigating towards an area filled with moderately good options rather than an area with mostly terrible outcomes and a single great one. This navigation could be through physical spatial dimensions (e.g., driverless vehicles), or through a metaphorical plane of possible outcomes over time (e.g., medical decision making). To do this, we need a Leximin algorithm that assigns moral *weights* to actions rather than just picking one and discarding the rest. To do this, we need to take the idea of a landscape more literally.

The most important concept from the last 200 years of physics is the idea of a *field*. Fields are entities that have a value for every point in time and space. For example, in the 61B café where I'm writing this right now, there is a value for the temperature at every point in the room, so we might call this a "temperature field." There's only one number for every point in the field (the temperature measurement), so it's a scalar field. Outside the café, the wind is blowing fiercely, and there's a value for the wind strength and direction at every point in the air, which could be called a "wind field." There are two values for this field (which direction the wind is blowing and how strong it's blowing), so it's called a *vector field*. The temperature field and the wind field are importantly related (since changes in temperature are what cause wind), so we could take these two fields and lay them on top of each other to see the way that the values in temperature correlate with the values in wind. In the nineteenth century, the term *field* was coined by Michael Faraday to describe the electromagnetic force, and even today the familiar diagrams of magnetic fields are what most of us imagine when we hear this term. But what's made the idea so central to physics is that it turns out just about every physical entity can be described as a field, from gravitational fields to electron fields. It's easy to create a field of your own: just make a grid on the floor and write a number on each square of the grid. Behold, you've made a field!

Why would we want to make a field? Imagine you have a flat rubber surface and you want to roll a marble so that it lands right in the middle of the sheet. If you don't have good aim, an easy way to do this is to pull the rubber sheet down right at the middle, and roll the marble in that direction. By pulling down the rubber sheet, you've made a field where each point on the sheet has a value for steepness. Steepness has a magnitude and a direction, so this is a vector field. A marble moving in a constant velocity through this steepness field is following a simple procedure of moving to a larger steepness than the current position, which is called "gradient descent." Because the middle of the sheet has the largest depth, a marble moving with constant velocity will eventually fall right into the middle and stop. Pulling down on a rubber sheet creates an attractive field for the marble (Figure 6.5a). If you can't physically pull down the sheet, you could simulate this effect by drawing a grid on the sheet and writing a steepness value for each point on the grid, which might look like a big set of arrows that get larger and larger towards the middle. Some methods for robot navigation use this approach for moving towards a goal. If the robot is following a simple gradient descent procedure, it will eventually reach the goal and stop, just like the marble.

Imagine now that there are lots of obstacles on the rubber sheet that you want the marble to avoid on its path towards the center. One intuitive way of doing this is to pull the sheet *up* around these obstacles, just like you pulled the sheet down at the middle. If the field we create by pulling down on the sheet is attractive, the one we create by pulling up on the sheet is repulsive (Figure 6.5b).

Combining these two fields together creates the same result as pulling down on the middle of the rubber sheet and pulling up around the obstacles: we've created a field with both attractive and repulsive forces. Just like water flowing around mountains and towards a canyon, the marble following the gradient descent will effortlessly swerve around these objects and towards the goal (Figure 6.5c).

In our rubber sheet, if you want to move the marble to the middle faster, you can pull the sheet down more at the middle, creating higher attractive steepness. Similarly, if you are more scared of one obstacle than another, you can pull the sheet up higher around the scarier one, creating higher repulsive steepness.

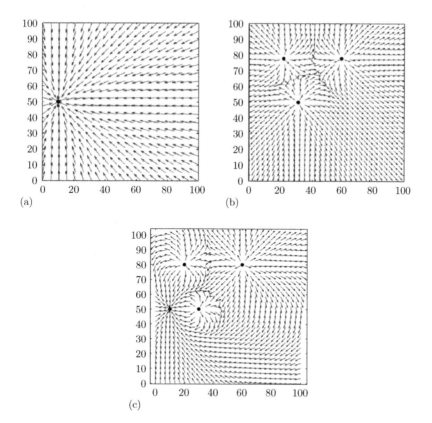

FIGURE 6.5 Examples of an attractive field around a single point (a), repulsive fields around three points (b), and the sum of the two fields (c).

Let's assign each obstacle a repulsive steepness based on its Leximin value: how harmful that outcome is for the worst-off person. Then our object will avoid the worse outcomes more (Figure 6.6).

So far, we've been using a measurement of primary goods where higher numbers are *better*. However, if we're creating a repulsive field around outcomes, then higher numbers should be connected to *worse* outcomes. For example, if our minimum values are: (2, 3, 1, 3), we want 1 to have the highest repulsive value, and 3 to have the lowest. If the values are on a set scale, like likelihood of survival, then we could just assign each action a weight equal to the inverse of its Leximin value, which in this case would be likelihood of death. Another way is to bake this directly into the data itself, changing the measurement system so that higher numbers equal worse payoffs of primary goods. In an ethics engine for driverless vehicles, we could say that the number 30 represents a 30 percent chance of dying in a collision instead of a 30 percent chance of surviving the collision. Now, we run a simple MAX procedure to find out which action has the highest probability of death for the worst-off person. These would be the values for our landscape, which could be called a "harm field." Points with no obstacles

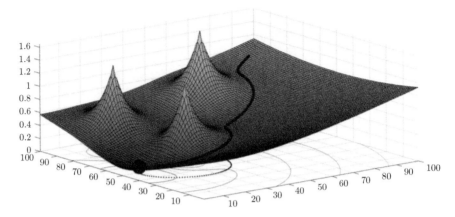

FIGURE 6.6   Simple gradient descent through the 3-D surface of a potential field like the one in Figure 6.5.

will have values near zero; points with more danger for the worst-off patients will have higher values.

If we're adding together the attractive field of goals to the repulsive field of harm, it's possible that strong enough goals might negate the strength of obligations. Think of the way that the force of a magnetic field can overwhelm the force of the gravitational field when a magnet pulls metal off the ground. But this seems contrary to the "categorical" property of moral obligations, where the mere desires of an individual can never excuse an agent from her duties. As discussed in Chapters 2 and 4, this is a bullet that I think Contractarianism needs to bite; it's almost always in your self-interest to act morally, but in rare exceptions, it can be in your self-interest to act immorally. This doesn't mean morality ceases to apply. In the context of our moral landscape, the repulsive force of moral obligations still *exists* and still *acts* on the behavior of an agent, but the force of obligation just fails to overwhelm the attractive forces of selfishness in certain rare cases where exploitation of others can be guaranteed. This is not creating homogeneous interests, like some collective mind (think of the Borg from *Star Trek*). Instead, caring about morality is simultaneously caring about your own interests within the constraints of ensuring that you're not gaining from the losses of others. In humans, moral grammar is a patch that has been added on to our preexisting self-interests. But in designing ethical robots, we can hardwire a genuine concern for ethics into its interests from the start.

Misunderstandings

Like any topic that's been through the popular media, there are confusions about the moral problems presented by autonomous vehicles. This section will consider three misunderstandings about this topic, some of which have already been mentioned, but it's worth repeating.

#1: Most moral principles will generate the same behavior, with only minor differences in extreme conditions

… However, small effects can add up over time.

A philosopher, an engineer, and a Contractarian walk into a bar. The philosopher says: "Moral theories will have a big influence on vehicle behavior in moral dilemma situations. It could mean the difference between crashing into a wall or plowing into a crowd of pedestrians." The engineer says: "These scenarios are rare, and even when they occur, moral principles will not have any significant effect on the behavior of the vehicle. We can just ignore these moral theories and build a vehicle that always decelerates and tries to avoid collisions, no matter what." They're both wrong, but since I'm sitting with them, I'll be polite and say that they're both partly correct. The engineer is correct that these situations are extremely rare, and the goal of autonomous vehicles should be avoiding collisions entirely. Focusing too much on situations like these may give the public an exaggerated idea of how frequently they encounter situations where every path leads to a collision. On the other hand, a driverless vehicle will constantly need to be evaluating collisions to make minor adjustments in direction and speed, and small differences can add up over massive scales. Just swerving slightly closer towards a wall rather than the bus could make a large difference over billions and trillions of iterations. Considering these extreme cases will be helpful in evaluating the long-term consequences of driverless vehicle behavior. As I suggested, thinking about cases like the probabilistic trolley dilemma can help determine how to integrate the expected harm and likelihood of collision. And comparing different moral principles can demonstrate the long-term effects of autonomous vehicles over trillions of vehicle interactions.

#2: It's only morally acceptable to use physical information about people to evaluate collisions, not social information

In 2016, researchers at MIT released an online interactive game called Moral Machine, where players get to make decisions in trolley-style dilemmas involving driverless cars. The website described the game as follows:

> The Moral Machine is a platform for gathering a human perspective on moral decisions made by machine intelligence, such as self-driving cars. We generate moral dilemmas, where a driverless car must choose the lesser of two evils, such as killing two passengers or five pedestrians. As an outside observer, people judge which outcome they think is more acceptable. They can then see how their responses compare with other people.

This sounds like the same old trolley dilemma, but in this version the dependent variable isn't whether one is acting directly to kill one person. Instead, the variables are demographic facts about the potential victims. Some characters

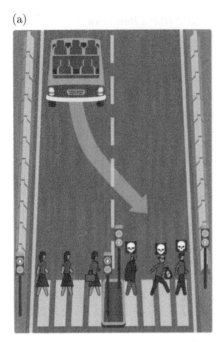 

FIGURE 6.7 A screenshot from the MIT "Moral Machine" game. The scenario is a "self-driving car with sudden brake failure" that must choose between two deadly paths. Players are forced to choose between swerving to kill a homeless person, a criminal, and a man (a) or going straight to kill two women and a female executive (b). This kind of information is unacceptable to use in making moral decisions.

are described (and *pictured*) as being overweight, homeless, criminals, athletes, doctors, and so on (Figure 6.7).

As we saw in Chapters 4–5, physical facts about a person are relevant from the original position, but social facts like their race, religion, gender, and sexual orientation are not. By using social properties as their criteria for moral decision making, this experiment is mistakenly testing people's discriminatory biases rather than their moral judgments. Imagine that the game included descriptions of race, religion, and sexual orientation. The MIT researchers don't want to ask: "Are you willing to sacrifice the lives of three gay women to save a Muslim?" But what they're doing in asking about class and occupation is essentially the same thing. Any student who's taken an introductory ethics class understands why this game is not only misguided but dangerous.

#3: Driverless vehicles will not "target" people or vehicles

One objection to both utilitarian and Contractarian principles is that they unfairly *target* safer drivers and vehicles, because collisions with these objects produce less overall harm and reduce the worst possible harm. In a recent article in *Slate* magazine, Jesse Kirkpatrick warned that motorcyclists who wear helmets are essentially being penalized and discriminated against for their responsible decision to wear a helmet:

> [I]t seems unfair to penalize motorcyclists who wear helmets by programming cars to strike them over non-helmet wearers, particularly in cases where helmet use is a matter of law. Furthermore, it is good public policy to encourage helmet use; they reduce fatalities by 22–42 percent, according to a National Highway Traffic Safety Administration report. As a motorcyclist myself, I may decide not to wear a helmet if I know that crash optimization algorithms are programmed to hit me when wearing my helmet. We certainly wouldn't want to create such perverse incentives.

The same objection could be raised for safe cars: if a vehicle must decide between colliding with two vehicles, where one has a higher safety rating than the other, the vehicle will prefer colliding with the safer one (the occupant has a higher probability of survival). Isn't this unfair, and won't it incentivize people to be less safe to avoid becoming targets of ethics algorithms?

This point is really two objections: a moral one (it's unfair to punish people for being safe) and a practical one (this will incentivize people to be less safe). Let's get rid of the practical objection, because it's just silly. There is absolutely no risk that people are going to stop wearing helmets and buying safer cars to avoid becoming targets of driverless vehicles. Dilemma situations like the trolley problem are *extremely* rare; it's *astronomically* more probable that a person will be involved in a normal collision than a dilemma-style collision. Any safety device brings with it some small risk. Not wearing a helmet or buying a less safe car because you're worried about being targeted by an ethics algorithm would be like deciding not to wear a seat belt because they occasionally can lead to harm or death. Seat belts are much more likely to save you than kill you, although there is some small chance of the latter. Similarly, helmets and safe cars are much more likely to save you than result in you being targeted by a crash optimization program, although there is some small chance of the latter. So there's no practical reason why ethics algorithms would lead to less public safety.

However, the fairness objection still stands: isn't this *punishing or targeting* people for being safe? The problem here is using terms like "punish" and "target," which are clearly not the purpose of the algorithm. It's misleading to say that a vehicle is programmed to *hit*, *target*, or *punish* anybody. Even if it produces the same results as punishment, we've seen in the first chapter that whether an action is perceived as punishment depends on the intention of the punisher. If your car's brakes fail and you accidentally run over a terrorist who has just killed thousands of people, this might have the same effect as if you had intentionally run him over, but most of us would not describe the accidental death as an act of *punishment*. The algorithm we're using is never programmed to harm. Instead, it's programmed to prefer the highest minimum survival value to the lowest minimum survival values. Using active terms like *hit* and *target* suggests that this is the goal or intention of the program, and gives the impression of unfairness. If Leximin really is the procedure that's optimal from the original position, then it is, by definition, the fair judgment.

Chapter summary

- A moral dilemma for an autonomous vehicle occurs whenever every path crosses into the "danger cone" of another obstacle. It's theoretically possible for a network of autonomous vehicles in ideal circumstances to avoid moral dilemmas entirely. However, even if these scenarios constitute a small percentage of vehicle interactions, they could result in thousands of injuries or deaths per year.
- Collisions must be evaluated by their magnitude as well as their likelihood. According to Contractarianism, the relevant primary good in vehicle collisions is health and survival.
- A Contractarian ethics engine would assess collisions using factors like relative velocity and angle of impact to generate an "h-value" (harm value) in vehicle collisions. This could be generated from a sufficiently large database of severe injuries in collisions.
- The Leximin principle will select those paths which maximize the worst h-values, as opposed to other principles which will select paths with the best sum of h-values, or only consider the h-values of the driver.
- One simple implementation of the Contractarian ethics engine for vehicle navigation systems is using a potential field approach, where obstacles are assigned repulsive values based on the worst h-values in each collision.
- There are several misunderstandings about the ethics of autonomous vehicles: (1) Even if moral dilemmas constitute a small fraction of vehicle collisions, they are important to plan for. (2) Driverless vehicles must not use social-relational information in evaluating collisions. (3) It's misleading to characterize vehicles as "punishing" or "targeting" people, since the primary goal of the system is to create a fair distribution among all players regardless of their current standing.

Notes

1 I hear my inner mathematician saying: "Technically these aren't really cones! A cone is a three-dimensional object, but these are 2-D slices of cones, called *conic sections*." Luckily, I'm not a mathematician, so I don't have to listen to this voice. We'll just call them cones.
2 In Park and Kuipers's model, the amount of red on a path indicates the likelihood of collision, with more likely collisions having more red than green.
3 You might be skeptical about setting up such a one-dimensional scale of health, with probability of survival being the proxy measurement. After all, survival might not have the same value when translated along the dimensions of age or social importance. A 50 percent probability of a 90-year-old person surviving might have a different

value than a 50 percent probability of a 5-year-old surviving. A 50 percent probability of a person with an untreatable and terminal disease might have a different value than a 50 percent probability of a young and healthy person surviving. Even within the original position, there's a plausible argument that, not knowing which person you would be, any self-interested person from behind the veil of ignorance would favor the survival of someone with more "quality-adjusted life years" (QALY) remaining in their lifetime over one with fewer (I'm aware that this is skating on thin ice, from a Rawlsian perspective). QALYs are a common tool for determining the allocation of scarce medical resources. If a computer were able to take into account the ages and health information of all the potential victims and run these into a function of remaining QALYs, then these values could be used as coefficients to weight the probabilities of survival. For example, if the probabilities of survival for Player A and B are: (0.5, 0.8), but their remaining QALYs are: (30, 5), then their resultant values would be: ((0.5)(30), (0.8)(5)) = (15, 4). In this scenario, even though Player B has a higher probability of survival, Player A would have the higher health value when QALYs are factored into the calculation.

There is some reason to be hesitant about the use of QALYs in the Leximin calculation. There are already many moral objections to the use of QALYs to allocate scarce medical resources, and I suspect that there would be public outrage to the idea that every person is attached a value based on their health that could be used to weigh human lives. As I hinted at, this is also skating on thin ice from a Rawlsian perspective, because it comes dangerously close to using social value as a factor in weighing lives. There are already rampant misunderstandings in the way that we should approach trolley problems: MIT's Moral Machine sets up trolley dilemmas where a driverless car must choose between killing people based on information about the victims' weight, gender, employment, and criminal history. We've seen that a Rawlsian (or any moral theorist, for that matter) would be aggressively opposed to this, for obvious reasons. Although the use of QALYs is still justifiable from the original position, it might be more politically risky than the use of bare survival probabilities.

References

Choset, Howie & Lynch, Kevin & Huchinson, Seth & Kantor, George & Burgard, Wolfram & Kavraki, Lydia & Thrun, Sebastian (2005). *Principles of Robot Motion: Theory, Algorithms, and Implementation.* Cambridge, MA: MIT Press.

Fraichard, Thierry & Asama, Hajime (2004). "Inevitable Collision States – A Step towards Closer Robots?" *Advanced Robotics,* 18, 1001–1024.

Harris, Sam (2011). *The Moral Landscape: How Science Can Determine Human Values.* New York: Free Press.

Kirkpatrick, Jesse (2016). "The Ethical Quandary of Self-Driving Cars." *Slate,* June 6.

Lipson, Hod & Kurman, Melba (2016). *Driverless: Intelligent Cars and the Road Ahead.* Cambridge, MA: MIT Press.

Park, Jong Jin (2016). *Graceful Navigation for Mobile Robots in Dynamic and Uncertain Environments.* Ph.D. dissertation, University of Michigan, Ann Arbor.

7

SAVING LIVES

In Japan, there is a word for when an elderly person dies alone: *kodokushi*, or "lonely death." Unfortunately, this is a growing problem all over the world, causing perhaps 30,000 deaths per year in Japan alone. As the population of elderly people living alone rises, so will kodokushi. According to the U.S. Census Bureau, the proportion of the American population over the age of 65 has risen from 4.1 percent in 1900 to 13 percent in 2010, and is expected to reach 20.9 percent of the population by 2050. This trend is found in industrialized and postindustrialized countries all over the world. South Korea's elderly population has jumped from just 2.9 percent in 1950 to 12.7 percent in 2014, and is predicted to reach 40.1 percent in 2050. In Japan, the country with the highest elderly population, it has jumped from 6 percent in 1960 to 25.9 percent currently, and is also expected to reach 40 percent by 2050. One of the most obvious consequences of the aging boom has been a massive increase in the demand for healthcare. But a less obvious problem is *connecting* elderly people to healthcare. According to Daniel Kaplan at Cornell's Institute of Geriatric Psychiatry, "nearly 29% of the 46 million community-dwelling elderly live alone," and those who live alone are more likely to be poor, undernourished, experiencing depression and loneliness, and having difficulty keeping up with treatment regimens. At the same time, 90 percent of elderly people report a desire to maintain their independence. These are the causes of kodokushi. Just like deaths in car crashes, many people have accepted these deaths as an unfortunate but inevitable side-effect of the world we live in. However, most of these deaths may be preventable.

In 2013, Japan's budget allocated 2.3 billion yen to developing *carebots*, which are autonomous robots that provide comfort and assistance to the elderly. Companies like Toyota, Hyundai, and IBM have been racing towards providing carebots. IBM's prototype robot, the Multi-Purpose Eldercare Robot Assistant (MERA), is currently being developed with sensors that can read vital signs and detect

(a) (b) (c)

FIGURE 7.1 Three examples of carebots: IBM's Mera (a), RIKEN's Robobear (b), and BlueFrog's BUDDY (c). None of them are currently equipped with life-saving capacities, but if they were, an ethics engine would be necessary.

when a person has fallen. Japan's RIKEN institute has developed the Robobear nurse capable of lifting patients and taking them comfortably where they need to go. Companion robots like BlueFrog's BUDDY can remind people to take their medication and help them communicate with people via phone or video chat (Figure 7.1). As far as I'm aware, none of these carebots are currently equipped with lifesaving technologies like defibrillators and respirators, and none of them provide medications or injections; they just provide reminders. If carebots can be equipped with emergency life-saving equipment, we may have a moral obligation to the thousands of elderly people dying alone to try to build carebots that can provide a full spectrum of diagnosis, treatment, and care options.

Bioethics is one of the most important applications of moral philosophy, because making medical decisions almost always involves a trade-off between short-term harm versus long-term health, or prioritizing the health of one group at cost to another. Once robots begin to make autonomous decisions about when to provide patients with injections, medications, and other life-saving treatments, they will need to be equipped with an ethics engine. This chapter will describe how the Contractarian ethics engine would apply to autonomous robots that might typically live with elderly people and provide treatments for maintaining normal physical functioning. This includes keeping track of vital signs, food and water intake, respiration, assisting with meals and bathroom use, and administering prescribed medications, injections, and life-saving emergency treatments. We'll also see how the ethics engine applies to robots in emergency rescue situations like natural disasters, evacuations, and distributions of scarce medical resources like flu vaccines.

Obtaining consent to treatment

In bioethics, the most important principles are *beneficence* and *autonomy*. Beneficence is ensuring that your actions are always in the interests of maximizing the patient's well-being, while autonomy ensures that you always respect a patient's rights to control her own health outcomes. Both of these principles follow from our Contractarian moral theory, so our ethics engine will always produce behavior consistent with them. The Leximin algorithm ensures that every action maximizes the primary goods of the relevant players, and the consensual override ensures that any decision involving a *trade-off* of primary goods must always be confirmed with the worst-off person, assuming there's enough time. For autonomous vehicles making split-second decisions before car crashes, there isn't enough time to confirm the trade-offs inherent in moral dilemmas. But in medical decisions, there will almost always be time. For instance, even the most necessary surgery requires a trade-off in short-term harm (sedation, incisions, recovery) versus long-term health benefits. Leximin specifies when a necessary and life-saving surgery is the best option. Almost always, there will be enough time to adequately inform the patient about their medical problem, the available treatment options, their probable outcomes, and confirm the patient's wishes to move forward with treatment. If the patient expresses a genuine refusal of treatment, a medical robot must refrain from treatment. When a medical robot discovers that a patient needs her appendix removed immediately, we obviously don't want the robot to just start sedating the patient and going to work.

There are two exceptions where consent would not be required by healthcare robots. The first category includes health procedures that involve *no* trade-offs in health outcomes, meaning no patients experience any loss of health, but only benefits. I have in mind services like changing a person's bedsheets, filtering their air and water, changing the bedpan, keeping plates and silverware clean, and maintaining access to toilets. Our ethics algorithm does not require consent for these kinds of activities. Nurses don't typically ask a patient's consent to change the sheets or empty the bedpan. Of course, if a patient explicitly states that she doesn't want filtered water, the robot must respect her wishes, since she's the only one affected by the decision. But these sorts of typical nursing activities largely present no moral challenges.

The second exception to the consent override is emergency medicine, where most bioethicists agree that informed consent is implausible; there's not enough time to adequately inform patients about their options, and patients are often unconscious or incompetent. If there's no way to adequately confirm consent, then the default decision of the ethics engine will be to select the output of Leximin, which in this context will seek to maximize the overall health of the patient. Some of the most difficult challenges in bioethics involve cases where patients are incompetent to make medical decisions for themselves. For example, consider the case of Mary Northern, a 72-year-old Tennessee woman who developed gangrene in both of her feet. The medical staff at Nashville General Hospital informed her that she needed to have both her feet amputated, but she refused. The doctors decided that she was not competent to make medical decisions for herself, and she was assessed by a psychiatrist and two judges in the hospital. As one judge remarked in the transcripts, this was a very difficult case, because Ms. Northern appeared to be otherwise very competent, but in denial about the nature and extent of her disease. Doctors and nurses face cases like this all the time: patients who are able to communicate and articulate their wishes very clearly, but seem to not understand their disease and its consequences, or who refuse to think about it. How do we decide when patients are competent to provide consent?

A safe (and thus Maximin) strategy would be to err on the side of respecting consent. It's difficult enough for doctors, lawyers, psychiatrists, and judges to determine when a person is incompetent to make medical decisions, let alone design a machine that can do this, even with potentially unlimited amounts of data. The safest criterion for incompetence is being unconscious or otherwise unable to respond, and this should be the standard for autonomous medical robots. Otherwise, if a patient has the ability to provide an explicit request, this request should always be respected. Thus, if our carebot were to discover gangrene in Mary Northern's feet, it would first try to inform her of the diagnosis and the recommended treatment of amputation. If she was not capable of responding, it would call for an ambulance. If the ambulance couldn't get there in time, it might perform the surgery and save her life. If she can respond and clearly insists: "Don't call an ambulance, I don't want any doctors messing with my feet," the carebot would be obligated to do nothing.

This conclusion might sound extremely counterintuitive, but the paternalist position also has counterintuitive predictions as well. An excellent thought-experiment to illustrate the importance of medical consent was introduced by the philosopher Alvin Goldman (1970) in his article, "The Refutation of Medical Paternalism." I've paraphrased the scenario here:

> You meet a man named Bill at a train station (moral dilemmas all seem to involve trains). Bill tells you that he is going to New York for a very important meeting that will make or break his entire career. Later, you see him on the platform, but he's heading towards the wrong train! He's getting on the train to Boston, which is on the track opposite the train leaving for New York. You try yelling at him, "Bill! You're getting on the wrong train!" but it's no use, the platform is too noisy, nobody can hear a thing. You rush over to Bill and grab him, trying to show him that he's on the wrong train, but Bill just shouts "Hey! Get off me!" The only choices are to let him stay on the wrong train or drag him against his will over to the right train and throw him in it.

Goldman seems to think it's obvious that we should refrain from forcing Bill on the correct train, even if it's "for his own good." Over the years, I've found interesting disagreement across surveys of hundreds of student responses. Most of them disagree with Goldman, and think it's a good idea to throw Bill on the train to New York, under the assumption that it's what Bill *really* wants. "He'll thank you later" is a common reply. However, others deny that it's permissible to violate Bill's consent, even if it makes him worse-off overall. This is yet another place where moral intuitions diverge, and it's not clear based on principles like the Intentional Harm Rule or Tit-for-Tat exactly which action is "harm." Moral theories can do better: Utilitarianism says it's permissible to throw Bill on the correct train, while more deontological theories see it as an unacceptable violation of rights. If Contractarianism is the correct moral theory, then we must respect Bill's updated preference report, since moving him would be an action that lowers Bill's opportunity (by restricting his mobility) to benefit his secondary goals, namely, getting to New York. Since Bill is the worst-off person in every action (assume nobody else is realistically affected), we need his consent to take an action that restricts his mobility. In this situation, if he doesn't consent, a robot must allow him to board the wrong train.

Applying this thought-experiment to the domain of medicine produces scenarios like the following:

> A patient is brought into the emergency room who needs a blood transfusion to survive, but she insists that it's against her religion, and she would rather die. After she becomes unconscious, Dr. House realizes he can quickly give her a blood transfusion without her ever knowing and then pretend it was prayer that saved her life.

Students are also usually split about this case. What these scenarios reveal is that some people prefer religious goods over their own health, while others don't. I can say, "That's not how I would value those goods," but as I've conceded, there's no objective grounds for criticizing another's preferences. They must be based entirely on the actual or implied consent of the individuals. Goldman is correct that paternalism must be rejected in all its forms. We can use methods like the original position to predict someone's preferences, but consent is always an overriding method for updating these preferences.

Diagnosing and informing

How many people in the world die of easily diagnosed and treatable diseases? According to the World Health Organization, the leading causes of death in poor countries are:

- Lower respiratory infections
- Diarrheal disease
- Stroke
- Ischemic heart disease
- HIV/Aids
- Tuberculosis
- Malaria
- Preterm birth complications
- Birth asphyxia and birth trauma
- Road injury.

Examining the list of leading causes of death in wealthy countries, you won't find diarrheal tuberculosis, malaria, or complications during childbirth, because these are easily preventable with modern medicine. The reason that people in poor regions die from malaria is not only a lack of resources but also a lack of medical staff and expertise. Even with programs like Doctors Without Borders, some regions are either too dangerous or too undesirable to attract well-trained physicians. Once autonomous machines are capable of making accurate diagnoses of common diseases and injuries, as well as providing reliable and safe treatments, these carebots have the potential to save lives on a massive scale.

There's no obvious technical obstacle to machines providing diagnosis and treatment independently of human supervision. In 2011, the IBM computer called Watson defeated Ken Jennings and Brad Rutter in the game show *Jeopardy!* Soon afterwards, the company announced that Watson would soon be directed at assisting with medical diagnosis. In an interview with IEEE Spectrum, Robert Wachter from UC San Francisco Medical Center notes that "They [IBM] are making some headway," but nothing yet like the better-than-human performance that we were hoping for. Other programs have also been developed for diagnostics, like Isabel and DXplain, and both have been endorsed by the American Medical Association. Despite the slow start, progress in robotic medical diagnosis is happening. For example, in a 2017 paper published in *PLOS One*, Stephen Wang and colleagues demonstrated that a machine learning algorithm trained on data from 378,256 patients could effectively predict cardiovascular events at a rate much higher than the current methods for prediction. Even if this progress is slower than expected, the fact that medical diagnosis is nothing more than a conditional probability inference based on symptoms and medical history suggests that machines will eventually surpass humans in this skill, just like chess and *Jeopardy!*. Just like driverless vehicles, medical robots should not be available to the general public until their performance in diagnosis and treatment is better than human performance, maybe even several times better.

On the side of treatment, machines are already used by many hospitals to provide more accurate and safe surgical procedures than human surgeons alone. In 2000, the FDA approved the use of the da Vinci surgical system, which allows a surgeon to make smaller and more precise incisions and sutures with the aid of cameras and robotic arms that she controls manually. It's not an autonomous robot, since the actions are collaboratively made by the machine and a human surgeon; the company's website promises: "Your surgeon is 100% in control of the *da Vinci* System at all times. *da Vinci* technology translates your surgeon's hand movements into smaller, precise movements of tiny instruments inside your body." However, more autonomous surgical robots are currently being developed. In 2016, Azad Shademan and colleagues published research demonstrating a robot that performs better than human surgeons in a procedure called intestinal anastomosis (carried out on a pig intestine). There's no reason to doubt that machines will eventually surpass human physicians in any kind of medical procedure.

Once carebots surpass humans in their ability to diagnose diseases and carry out a wide range of treatments, from prescribing medication to performing surgery, what are the moral challenges that they will face? Many of them are the same as those described earlier in the chapter: ensuring that the patient's health is maximized, while her consent is simultaneously respected at all times. In addition, because doctors are providing information to patients, they have an additional responsibility to be clear and educational in their interactions with patients. Access to information is a primary good, as I've argued, but *access* doesn't just mean exposure. I can show a patient some set of information in a language she doesn't understand, but this is restricting her opportunities more than translating them into her native language. One benefit of robotic physicians is that they have the potential to speak and understand *every* human language, which can overcome many of the translation challenges that doctors often face in multiethnic regions. However, even if a robot presents data in the relevant language, medical terminology is a language all on its own that most people find frighteningly incomprehensible. Imagine a patient asks an autonomous robot for diagnosis and the robot replies:

> The most likely cause of your symptoms is viral gastroenteritis, with a 93 percent confidence level, followed by endrometriosis, with a 3 percent confidence level, giardiasis with a 2 percent confidence level, and gastric volvus with a 1 percent confidence level. Each of these has a less than 0.1 percent chance of mortality, except for gastric volvus, which has a 17.5 percent chance of mortality.

Most people (myself included) would be confused and frustrated by a barrage of medical terms with likelihoods. A more helpful presentation would be a description of these diseases along with descriptions like "very likely" and "moderately life-threatening."

Another challenge in presenting treatment options is that humans are often biased and poorly informed, especially when it comes to statistics and probability. As demonstrated by Daniel Kahneman and Amos Tversky, the way that information is framed and anchored can have large effects on the decisions that people make. If a college student is considering whether to play American football in the NFL, his doctor might tell him that he has a 14 percent chance of developing Alzheimer's disease after playing in the NFL, which could discourage him. Or, the doctor could tell him that he has an 86 percent chance of having no negative cognitive effects from playing in the NFL, which might sway him to the other side (this is called a framing effect). Telling him that the rate of Alzheimer's amongst NFL players is almost 1.5 times higher than the normal population makes it sound bad, but saying that it's only 4 percent higher than the general population makes it sound better (this is an anchoring effect). All of these statements are true, but they're phrased in a way to change our perception of the risks. So how should robots convey information to people about their choices in a way that doesn't bias their decisions? Just as for human physicians, I don't think there's an easy answer. It would be nice to say: "Just give people the facts," but facts need to be expressed in a comprehensible way. Handing someone an Excel sheet with the numbers on it will only create confusion, and a sigh of: "Oh, you just tell me what's best." Obviously, the raw data about threats and outcomes should be available to people, but there should also be an effort among engineers and computer scientists to convey this information in a way that balances simplicity with neutrality.

One objection that could be raised to carebots is that they can provide information to patients, but not *guidance*. In some models of the doctor-patient relationship, like those described by bioethicists Ezekiel and Linda Emanuel (1992), a physician ought to develop a relationship with the patient and provide her own recommendations about treatment options based on this relationship. This involves a negotiation between what the doctor thinks is best and would want for herself, and what the doctor interprets the patient as wanting and caring about. However, if a robot has no attitudes about what it would want, and it isn't able to interpret the patient's personal interests and values, then something essential may be left out if people are only interacting with robotic physicians.

This is a valid concern, and I agree that offering guidance and building a personal rapport are desirable traits for physicians. However, they are not necessarily obligations. Imagine a doctor like Hugh Laurie's character from the television show *House* who is cold and shows no interest in the patients' personal lives, but is accurate in his diagnoses and usually forthright about the treatment options. This is not the ideal doctor, but still a minimally acceptable one. In cases where ideally experienced and thoughtful doctors are unavailable, there's nothing wrong with introducing minimally acceptable ones. This argument applies to both robotic and human doctors.

Rescue principles

In the movie *I, Robot*, the main character (played by Will Smith) is in a car accident that sends both him and a young girl into a river. A robot that just happens to be nearby performs a quick calculation, and realizes that Smith's character has a greater chance of survival, so the robot dives into the water, saving him rather than the girl. After Smith's character is rescued, he is furious about this decision, and remarks that this is only the decision a *robot* would make. In this sense, Smith's character is probably right. Our evolved moral grammar is very sensitive to features like age and gender; in a scenario where only one person can be saved, people typically view it as better to save a woman over a man, and a child over an adult. In addition, most medical policies about the distribution of vaccinations during epidemics prioritize the most vulnerable members of a population before the less vulnerable ones. But, as we've seen, our evolved moral grammar can often lead to biased decisions, leading people to prioritize family members and in-groups over others without justification. In designing autonomous robots, we must ask: what rescue policy should we be programming?

Most moral theories, along with our intuitive moral grammar, break down in rescue situations, since every action results in some violation of "rights" or "consent." Unsurprisingly, people often come up with a rationalization for avoiding rescue decisions; the most common one is that deciding who lives and who dies is "playing God," implying that we should avoid the entire issue. Like most rationalizations, this can be easily dismissed by showing its absurdity in other contexts. The bioethicist Bonnie Steinbock (2006) points out many of these absurdities:

> All medical intervention is "Playing God," in the sense that human intervention is changing the course of nature. By vaccinating children, by treating people with antibiotics, and by transplanting organs, we prevent the deaths of millions of people each year ... It seems that each new medical intervention is regarded with suspicion, as a human transgression on divine prerogative. This is true of organ transplantation, which is now an accepted part of modern medicine.

Thus, even though rescue dilemmas are new and frightening situations that nobody wants to think about, if robots are going to have the abilities to intervene where humans aren't able to assist, they'll need to be programmed with principles for prioritizing who is rescued first.

Let's consider a real example of conflicting rescue principles. During the aftermath of Hurricane Katrina in 2005, the staff at Memorial Medical Hospital found themselves in a desperate crisis. The hospital was surrounded by floodwater, power was completely lost, and temperatures soared into triple digits. As described vividly by the journalist Sheri Fink in her book, *Five Days at Memorial* (2013), the doctors and nurses were forced to make agonizing life-and-death choices in their efforts to evacuate the hospital. The medical staff started off with a standard policy of giving the sickest and most vulnerable patients evacuation priority, but they quickly began to reverse this policy when it became clear that there were healthy people who might be potentially sacrificed in order to rescue those who were dying. The medical chairperson may have started this shift in policy when he decided that patients with DNRs would have lowest evacuation priority, later defending this on the grounds that these patients had "least to lose."

According to Fink, doctors like Dr. Ewing Cook and Dr. Anna Pou, who was later arrested for second-degree murder (but not indicted by a grand jury), eventually began hastening the deaths of patients who were lowest priority by increasing their dosage of drugs like morphine and the sedative Versed. All of this was done out of a sense that, according to Pou, not everyone would be able to be saved. Despite the controversy about whether this judgment was correct in the case of Memorial Hospital, this type of situation is common in the aftermath of natural disasters; decisions must be made about who has priority when not everyone can be saved. If the natural disaster is nuclear, as with the 2011 meltdown at the Fukushima Daiichi nuclear plant, robots may be the only safe way of evacuating people without risking more human lives in the process.

In their discussion of distributing scarce vaccinations during flu epidemics, the bioethicists Govind Persad, Alan Wertheimer, and Ezekiel Emanuel (2009) survey a number of principles that have historically been used in rescue situations to determine priority:

- Equality-based principles (e.g., lottery, first come first served)
- Saving the worst-off (e.g., sickest first, oldest first, youngest first)
- Maximizing total benefits (e.g., number of lives saved, save the healthiest).

Each of these principles has some precedent. Firefighters in burning buildings try to save the most lives, while doctors in emergency rooms follow the *first come first served* approach. Organ transplant boards favor the patients who are in the worst conditions, while American military doctors during WWII chose to distribute penicillin based on the soldiers who were most likely to recover. In the *I, Robot* scenario, principles like *save the worst off* or *save the most life-years* would prioritize the child, since she is the most vulnerable and has the most life ahead of her, all else being equal. Principles like *save the most likely to recover* might prioritize the adult, given that he has a greater chance of survival. Going against the usual conventions, Persad and his colleagues suggest distributing vaccinations to the healthy and young before those who are sick and old, under the assumption that they have more life-years ahead of them and more to lose.

Which of these rescue principles would our Contractarian ethics engine produce? It turns out that most of these principles find some place in the Contractarian view, depending on the situation. To illustrate, I'll present a number of rescue situations, modulating the relevant features of (1) prior health, (2) expected gains and losses, and (3) population.

The most vital (and often neglected) assumption in this discussion is that the expected values for each player must be the arithmetic *difference* between her current state and the predicted state. As discussed in Chapter 4, there are some good grounds for thinking that a rational agent from behind the veil of ignorance would be more concerned about a player who lost 50 units than a player who lost 5, even if the first player wound up with more total units than the second. This is the distinction between consequence-based moral theories and theories that take prior states into consideration. When applied to life and health, this implies that lowering the health of one person by 20 percent is morally worse than lowering the health of another by 10 percent, even if the former winds up being still much healthier than the latter.

In the simplest case where we must decide between two random people needing rescue from a burning building without any additional information, the Leximin outcome is easy to generate. Because we assume the prior states and potential losses are equal for both players, our ethics engine will randomize (Figure 7.2).

In this scenario, there are equal numbers of players in each group with equal potential losses and gains for both. However, let's now assume that the first group has only a single player (P1) while the second group has two players (P2 and P3).

Save Randomly

(Groups with identical populations and losses)

		P1 (group 1)	P2 (group 2)
Randomize	Prioritize Group 1	0	−99
	Prioritize Group 2	−99	0

FIGURE 7.2 A rescue-scenario where two groups have equal numbers and equal losses. Here, a payoff of 0 indicates no losses (and no gains), while a payoff of −99 means a 99 percent loss to survival likelihood. The Leximin procedure will randomize.

Each group faces the same potential gains and losses by being rescued or left behind. In this scenario, the Leximin principle will favor a "save the most lives" policy (Figure 7.3).

Thus, in dealing with individuals or groups who have indistinguishable prior health states and outcomes, Contractarianism will endorse a lottery principle in evenly paired groups and a save-the-most-lives principle in comparing larger with smaller groups.

Let's consider cases where groups have asymmetrical losses. When players have different prior health states or different losses, the save-the-most-lives principle disappears, since some of the people now qualify as worse-off than others. For example, in flu pandemics, the U.S. policy is to prioritize groups that are most vulnerable. During the H1N1 epidemic of 2009, the priority list included those whose health conditions might make them especially vulnerable to the effects of the flu, pregnant women, children, and the elderly. Assuming that the losses to vulnerable people are greater than the losses to healthy people, this is a principle that Leximin will also advocate (Figure 7.4).

This principle is justified whenever one player's prior states make her losses dramatically worse than the same losses to a more fortunate player. Imagine a lifeguard who must decide between saving two people, one of them is a relatively good swimmer and the other can't swim at all. It's obvious that neglecting the person who can't swim will doom them to almost certain death, while it's possible that the good swimmer might be able to tread water for some time before needing help. Here, prioritizing the good swimmer will almost certainly

Save the Most Lives

(Groups with different populations, but identical losses)

		P1 (group 1)	P2 (group 2)	P3 (group 2)
	Prioritize Group 1	0	−99	−99
✓	Prioritize Group 2	−99	0	0

FIGURE 7.3 A rescue scenario where Group 1 is composed of only P1, while Group 2 is composed of P2 and P3. Each group faces identical potential losses.

Save the Most Vulnerable

(Groups where healthy people are less affected)

		P1 (sick)	P2 (healthy)	P3 (healthy)
✓	Prioritize Sick	0	−50	−50
	Prioritize Healthy	−80	0	0

FIGURE 7.4 In rescue scenarios where healthy people are less affected, the Leximin procedure will prioritize the most vulnerable.

leave the other to die, while prioritizing the non-swimmer might still leave the other player with a 50 percent chance of survival. In this case, even if the non-swimmer started out at a higher prior health status, the amount that she stands to lose is far greater than the good swimmer. Where healthy people still have some decent chance of surviving, the Contractarian algorithm will now prioritize rescuing the older and sicker members of the group. I strongly suspect that most typical pandemic and rescue scenarios will be ones where a "save the most vulnerable" principle applies: healthier people will lose less by waiting. This may also account for our usual intuitions about prioritizing the older and sicker members of a group.

Finally, there are major public health risks where both healthy and sick people face the same risks. In cases like these, the Leximin will advocate prioritizing the healthiest over the most vulnerable. This is also the principle that Persad et al. endorse. According to the Leximin procedure, healthy people have "more to lose" in terms of the changes between their prior and current payoffs. According to the ethics engine I've defined, it's better to allow many (and potentially indefinite numbers of) sick people to die to save a younger and healthier person. The principle becomes *save the healthiest* (Figure 7.5).

It's only in the most extreme of emergency rescue situations, where those who are neglected are virtually guaranteed to die, that this principle may apply. In the example of Memorial Medical Center, this is exactly the change that happened in the minds of the doctors and nurses as they moved from reasoning about standard emergencies to extreme ones. Whether or not Memorial Medical Center was actually an extreme emergency situation is still a matter of debate. It's possible that the

Save the Healthiest

(Groups where healthy people are equally or more affected)

		P1 (sick)	P2 (healthy)	P3 (healthy)
	Prioritize Sick	0	−99	−99
✓	Prioritize Healthy	−30	0	0

FIGURE 7.5 In rescue scenarios where healthy people are equally or more affected, the Leximin procedure will prioritize the healthiest, on the grounds that they lose more when not prioritized (they have higher prior states).

medical faculty of the hospital misjudged how dire their situation really was. Most of the outrage from the public afterwards came not from their policies about prioritizing the healthiest patients but from the allegations of involuntary euthanasia. As we've seen, Contractarianism would never endorse involuntary euthanasia, since consent is always required for trade-offs in primary or secondary goods within an individual. However, the general policy of prioritizing the healthiest people in a catastrophic emergency is indeed endorsed by Leximin.

We've seen that the Contractarian ethics engine will generate different rescue principles depending on information about the players' prior states, likely losses, and the distribution of losses within the population. This may be intuitive to many readers, but it isn't merely an appeal to intuition. Instead, it follows directly from the Leximin algorithm that was proposed as an optimal solution to cooperation problems. This matching between theory and intuitions may be partly the result of our intuitions being evolved for the function of cooperation, and partly due to general reasoning about cooperative strategies in rescue situations.

Chapter summary

- The rapidly aging population of technologically advanced countries like South Korea, Japan, and the United States is creating a need for more sophisticated "carebots": autonomous medical robots that can make complex decisions about health outcomes.
- Carebots must be capable of respecting the consent of patients. Default values will be designed around primary goods: namely, actions that maximize optimal health outcomes (beneficence). When there is enough time to consult with a patient, and the patient is competent to understand the relevant outcomes, the carebot must always consult with the patient to confirm her preferences over the default goals of maximizing health.
- Doctor carebots that are responsible for diagnosing diseases and prescribing medications or surgeries must be capable of communicating information to the patient in a clear enough way that enables her informed consent. This will require a sophisticated level of natural language processing and emotional intelligence. It will also require an assessment of when the standard for patient competence is high or low (based on the severity of health outcomes).
- Search-and-rescue robots using a Contractarian ethics engine will follow a range of different principles depending on factors like the prior health states of the people involved and the number of people in each affected group. For decisions that result in identical losses to identical populations, Leximin will randomize. If a decision results in equivalent losses for different sized groups, then Leximin will save the most lives. In situations where healthy people have less to lose by a decision, Leximin will favour a prioritarian policy, while it will save the healthiest whenever healthy people will have the same outcomes as vulnerable members of the population.

References

Emanuel, Ezekiel & Emanuel, Linda (1992). "Four Models of the Physician-Patient Relationship." *Journal of the American Medical Association*, 267, 2221–2227.
Fink, Sheri (2013). *Five Days at Memorial: Life and Death in a Storm-ravaged Hospital.* New York: Ala Notable.
Goldman, Alvin (1970). "The Refutation of Medical Paternalism." Reprinted in B. Steinbock, A. Arras, & J. London (eds.) (2008). *Ethical Issues in Modern Medicine*, 7th edition. New York: McGraw-Hill.
Persad, Govind & Wertheimer, Alan & Emanuel, Ezekiel (2009). "Principles for Allocation of Scarce Medical Interventions." *The Lancet*, 373, 423–431.
Shademan, Azad & Decker, Ryan & Opfermann, Justin & Kim, Peter (2016). "Supervised Autonomous Robotic Soft Tissue Surgery." *Science and Translational Medicine*, 8, 337.
Steinbock, Bonnie (2006). "Reproductive Cloning: Another Look." *University of Chicago Legal Forum*, Vol. 2006, Article 4.
Weng, Stephen F. & Reps, Jenna & Kai, Joe & Garibaldi, Jonathan M. & Qureshi, Nadeem (2017). "Can Machine-Learning Improve Cardiovascular Risk Prediction Using Routine Clinical Data?" *PLOS One*, p. e0174944.

8
KEEPING THE PEACE

Here is an intentionally provocative thought-experiment. In the distant future, there is a police robot on every street corner, every passenger vehicle, and every room of every building in the world. These police robots are inactive most of the time and just sit in a corner like a large trash can or fire extinguisher, but they are activated when someone yells a keyword like "9-1-1 Help!" The police robots are programmed to detect when someone is actively causing harm or attempting to cause harm against other people. They don't categorize based on race, gender, religion, or any other relational properties. They carry no weapons (or possibly nonlethal ones like tasers), and they're made of a bulletproof material. Their goal is to identify anyone who is actively causing harm to another person's health, opportunity, or essential resources, and intervene to neutralize the threat in a way that causes as little damage as possible to the violent person. If these robots are fast and strong enough, they can quickly handcuff a person without any further violence, and then wait for further instructions and assistance. People can still engage in consensual violent behavior like boxing, rough sex, and extreme bingo, since the robots would only be activated when one person actively calls for help. Wherever you go in the world, there is a police robot within range of your voice, ready to protect you if you need it. Does this sound like a better world than the one we currently live in?

Your first objection might be: "This is a police state," but there are no new laws being created, and nobody actively surveilling your thoughts or behaviors in any way. All that's going on is speeding up the response time of emergency responders to essentially zero. Your next objection might be: "What if police robots don't correctly identify who is causing the harm?" This is a valid concern, but a sophisticated machine learning algorithm could probably identify aggressive and unwanted advances, and even if there is ambiguous behavior, the first action for a police robot would be to announce what it's doing and ask everybody to freeze, then ask each person if they're in need of assistance. In the case of children or actors who are play-fighting, it's easy for them to just tell the police robot that it was only a game and nobody is in trouble. The next objection might be: "Governments will take advantage of police robots to spy on people or control them." But if we open their programming to public scrutiny, it will be clear that the police robots aren't collecting any information unless they're activated, and can never interfere with anybody unless that person is actively causing a loss to the primary goods of others. "What about hacking or malfunctions?" Another good practical concern, but let's assume that the hardware and software in these police robots is virtually guaranteed to be invulnerable to hacks and will never break down. After all, we're just asking whether this ideal scenario would be better than our own world.

A widespread army of autonomous police robots sounds like a lot of money, effort, and risk. What are the possible benefits? An elimination of all violent crime everywhere in the world. No fear about travelling anywhere dangerous or being threatened. An end to bullying and intimidation. The elimination of police brutality and discrimination. No more rape, domestic abuse, or mass shootings. With all of these potential benefits, the answer to the question: "Is a world with perfectly functioning police robots a better one?" is obviously yes. But it's *not* obvious that the risks and costs of getting there are worth the benefits. Even if the risk of police robots is too high, the presence of at least *some* autonomous police robots might be enough to get massive decreases in crime, police brutality, and discrimination.

The moral challenge for police and military robots is: how to manage the correct response to a criminal or enemy who is actively threatening others? Contractarianism has some answers: optimize the predicted harm done to the victim against the harm caused in neutralizing the criminal. Importantly, a "criminal" or "enemy" will always be a person who is currently causing or is very likely to cause immediate moral harm, and this shouldn't be dependent on the laws or policies of any particular country. For humans, questions about the ethics of war are messy and complex, but this doesn't need to be the case for robots.

Police-bots

One of the rules in the U.S. Motion Picture Production Code established in the 1930s was that villains in movies must always be punished. Even though the motion picture code was abandoned in the 1960s in favor of the ratings system that is currently used, this rule is still followed implicitly by any studio that wants their movie to be a crowd-pleaser. No major American blockbuster would have a villain go unpunished, because people love to see bad guys get what they deserve. And by *love*, I mean people get real pleasure from it. It might offend you to think of getting pleasure from the suffering of others, but if the other person is perceived as deserving punishment, you will get pleasure from their suffering.

For example, here's a fun game that economists have played with volunteers for several decades now called *The Ultimatum Game:*

> Player A and Player B are randomly assigned the role of "proposer" and "responder." They know that these roles are completely random. Let's say that Player A is the proposer. This means that she is given some amount of money, like $10, which she gets to keep on one condition: she has to offer some of it to Player B. She can offer $5 and keep $5, or she can offer $2 and keep $8. She could even offer $0 and keep all of it, or offer $10 and keep nothing. That's her only move in the game. Player B is the responder, and he has only one move: accept the offer or reject it. If he accepts the offer, they both walk away with the money and never play this game again. If he rejects the offer, they both get nothing, and never play the game again. Either way, the point is that they will *never play again.*

Imagine that you are Player B in this game, and Player A offers you just $1, and keeps the rest. Would you accept or reject? Most students in my classes (and economics experiments) reject an offer like this. And the people who accept the offer are always shocked. When I ask people why they accept the offer, they act as if it's obvious: they have a choice of either $1 or $0, and some money is always better than nothing! According to traditional decision theory and game theory, this is correct; it doesn't make any sense to reject money for no possible gain. But people do it, and they *enjoy* doing it. Studies of people's neural and neurochemical responses in playing this game have consistently demonstrated that rejecting unfair offers creates a rush of excitement and pleasure that's just as real as any other pleasure (Gabay et al., 2014).

Punishment is a strange territory in ethics where everything seems upside-down. In most situations, causing harm to others is morally wrong, but in the context of punishment and self-defense, causing harm to others is morally permissible or maybe even required. Many soldiers become disturbed by this dizzying inversion: you're taught your entire life not to cause intentional harm to others, and now your job is causing intentional harm to others. The chief of mental health services for the Vermont VA told PBS in an interview:

> I think the loss of faith, both in the safety of the world and the loss of faith in one's own humanity, is threatened when people kill other people, which is what we train them to do in war. I mean, it's how you win the war is you kill people, but you take somebody off the street who spent their whole life learning not to kill other people, not to harm other people and put them in a situation where it's his job to kill somebody else. I've not ever met a person who killed others who was not affected by that.
>
> I was hearing a story from a World War II bomber the other day who talked about being able to see the people fleeing and still feeling that today – you know, "How could I have done such a thing? Where was my sense

of reason?" But we know how they did it. There are a lot of military training techniques which are based on dehumanizing the enemy and making people able to kill.

Punishment and war involve doing things that are viewed by most people as the worst actions you could ever perform, but in the context of war, they're rewarded and praised. What makes punishment and war so different that everything in ethics suddenly flips upside-down?

If our evolved moral grammar corresponds to a strategy in cooperation games like Tit-For-Tat, it's not surprising why people love punishment. Punishment is an essential part of the strategy. In the evolutionary dynamics of cooperation games, it's not enough to be nice on the first move and cooperative to cooperators, you also need to show your willingness to punish cheaters. This approach to punishment is called a *retribution* principle, which is based on retaliating for actions that occurred in the past, as opposed to looking towards the future. The retribution rule doesn't care about whether a cheater will cheat again or what the other effects of retaliation are. All it cares about is that a moral crime was committed, and the required rule is to punish. Moral philosophers have often written about punishment with a passion that verges on poetry. Here is John Locke (1689) on punishment:

> By breaking the law of nature, the offender declares himself to live by some rule other than that of reason and common fairness (which is the standard that God has set for the actions of men, for their mutual security); and so he becomes dangerous to mankind because he has disregarded and broken the tie that is meant to secure them from injury and violence. This is an offence against the whole human species, and against the peace and safety that the law of nature provides for the species.

When I read that phrase "an offence against the whole human species," it reminds me of the kind of overdramatic rage that wells up at minor offenses like being cut off in traffic. "This is an offence to the whole human species!" I yell in my head, or maybe out loud. There's a tendency to get carried away with zeal for punishment. Here is Immanuel Kant (1790) writing about what should happen if everyone in a society decided to consensually part ways and go off on their own:

> Even if a civil society resolved to dissolve itself with the consent of all its members – as might be supposed in the case of a people inhabiting an island resolving to separate and scatter themselves throughout the whole world – the last murderer lying in prison ought to be executed before the resolution was carried out. This ought to be done in order that every one may realize the desert of his deeds, and that blood-guiltiness may not remain upon the people; for otherwise they might all be regarded as participators in the murder as a public violation of justice.

Pause for a moment and consider what Kant is saying here: if the world were to end tomorrow, the first thing we should all do is to execute every murderer, so that we no longer have the "blood-guilt" of allowing guilty people to get away with their crimes. This is the position that revenge and punishment are not only permissible but morally required.

There's something satisfying about this kind of punishment that discards any kind of self-interest, but also something obviously irrational about it. The Ultimatum Game is useful because it shows how retribution-style punishment can lead to decisions that are obviously against everybody's interests, and serve no possible benefit. An alternative way of thinking about punishment is by looking forward to the future harms that will be prevented by punishing. This is called a *deterrence* principle, which is based on using force against cheaters to prevent them (and others) from cheating in the future. Usually when we think about the justification for things like traffic tickets and time-outs for children, the reason isn't to give a criminal something she deserves, but to try to guide people away from harmful actions. Think of the way that we treat animals which have harmed humans; most people don't scold a bear or yell "What an awful bear!" Instead, they either retrain the animal, move the animal somewhere that it can't harm people, or kill the animal. But none of these responses are typically registered as *punishing* the animal.

Moral philosophers who advocate a deterrence approach to punishment often point to how the *retributive* part of punishment can be explained as expressing a committed deterrence strategy. If you want to really prevent someone from cheating in a game, you show that you're committed to acting against your own self-interest with a cheater. "I'd rather we both lose!" Just like the Prisoner's Dilemma, this looks crazy from the perspective of a one-time game, but not from an indefinitely repeated game. If you're playing the Ultimatum Game with someone over and over again, then rejecting unfair offers can lead to the best outcome for you in the long run.

Let's try "switching into manual mode," as Joshua Greene suggests, and ask: what are the best ways of deterring violent behavior without the myopia of simple retribution-based strategies? According to Contractarianism, lowering the distribution of primary goods for one player is only justified to the extent that it makes the worst-off person better than she otherwise would have been. Imagine that a violent criminal is actively causing harmful battery to a victim during a robbery. In this case, it's clear that the victim is the worst-off person. There are many other distributions of goods that raise everybody up beyond the level of the person being assaulted, like the criminal being restrained. This *does* limit the criminal's opportunities, but not anywhere close to the amount that the victim's health was being lowered during the battery. Imagine a police-bot has three options: do nothing and allow the victim to be harmed, restrain the criminal without causing physical damage, or kill the criminal (Figure 8.1). These payoffs assume that the criminal doesn't get any improvements in health, opportunity, or essential resources from his crime, but that's because we could change this

Intervening in a Crime

States	P1 (victim)	P2 (criminal)
A1: Do nothing	−70	0
✓ A2: Restrain criminal	0	−10
A3: Kill criminal	0	−99

FIGURE 8.1 Three possible actions a police-bot might take during a violent crime.

number to any arbitrarily high value without any difference in the Leximin result. The Leximin procedure will prefer restraining the criminal.

These options are a simplification of a massive range of actions that could neutralize the threat to the victim, some of them causing more or less harm to the criminal. According to Leximin, the key is to make the criminal no worse off than the victim otherwise would have been. Just like all the other Leximin decisions, this is an optimization problem. The ideal action would be one that neutralizes the threat to the victim while causing no harm to the criminal. If warning the criminal will effectively prevent him from committing any future violence, this would be best of all.

What about nonviolent crimes, like littering? When John Locke uses the term "criminal," he means a rights-holder who violates the natural rights of others, and this is also what I have in mind. This is just the inverse definition of *innocent* from the first chapter. If you see someone littering and yell for our police-bots to intervene, a police robot might activate, fail to detect any nonconsensual harm to primary goods, and then deactivate. It's possible that we could program police robots to say: "Please don't litter," or even give someone a virtual fine, but restraints against a person's liberty are only justified when they are an active threat to the primary goods of others. Some jurisdictions famously have laws against strange and parochial actions like keeping holiday lights up too long and knitting during fishing season, but these are usually ignored by police officers for good reasons. Police, like soldiers, are often faced with making moral decisions about which laws they should and shouldn't enforce. From the original position, what we're concerned with policing are violent crimes that are *and should be* illegal.

You might worry about exactly what "active threat" means. In his classic text, *On Liberty* (1859), John Stuart Mill advocated freedom of thought and action so long as these don't cause direct physical harm to others. But he wrestled with the problem of what *direct* harm is. His famous example was inciting a riot; if you're making inflammatory remarks about a corn-dealer in private, that isn't likely to lead to immediate harm. On the other hand, when you're chanting: "Eliminate all corn-dealers!" to an angry mob in front of his house, this is much more likely to lead to immediate harm. This is an area ripe for machine learning algorithms. As discussed in Chapter 5, with a large enough database about actions that typically lead to harm, a learning algorithm can extract features of these actions and apply them to new situations with some degree of confidence. The higher the confidence that this action will lead to harm, the more justified the deterrence. After some high threshold of confidence that this action will almost certainly lead to harm, police robots would be justified in taking steps to restrain the threatening person.

As you can tell, this approach to designing police robots uses a deterrence principle rather than a retribution principle. The goal is to prevent immediate harms to the primary goods of others, rather than punishing people for past wrongs. In fact, a police robot would have no way of determining past wrongs. This is traditionally the role of the criminal justice system, rather than the police force. Their roles are importantly distinct; police officers are not supposed to make judgments about prior guilt. Police officers make local judgments in the present situation about people actively causing harm to others. It's true that police officers arrest people on the basis of warrants, but the purpose of this is to deliver those suspected of committing crimes to the criminal justice system for speedy trial. Let's turn to what a criminal justice system based on deterrence principles would look like, because this is an area where machines are already beginning to play a role in decision making.

Judge-bots

Many states like Michigan, Wisconsin, and Florida currently use an algorithm called COMPAS for determining whether a prisoner is likely to commit future crimes. COMPAS stands for "Correctional Offender Management Profiling for Alternative Sanction," and was developed by the company Northpointe, which was subsequently sold to a large Canadian software conglomerate. The algorithm uses information about a prisoner in categories like *criminal personality*, *social isolation*, *substance abuse*, and *residence/stability* to provide an estimate about how much risk this person presents to the safety of others. In 2012, New York State performed an evaluation that claimed the algorithm is 71 percent effective. Although the algorithm is only supposed to be a guide to decision making for judges and parole boards, its results are often cited as evidence. In 2013, Wisconsin resident Eric Loomis was sentenced to eight years in prison for stealing a car partly on the basis of his COMPAS score. Loomis challenged the use of this score as a violation of due process. Is there something wrong with the use of algorithms, or even judge and parole robots, in the criminal justice system?

To answer this, we have to step back and ask about the *purpose* of a criminal justice system. If courts and prisons are designed to bring retribution for past crimes, then it's hard to see how to program a machine to determine a proportional punishment. But then again, it's hard to see how *anybody* can determine what constitutes an appropriate punishment for a crime. The old cliché "an eye for an eye" fails in most non-eye related crimes, like rape and abuse. Do we rape a rapist, and abuse an abuser? A retribution approach might approve of these cruel and unusual punishments, but the Leximin principle says that this would be making the criminal just as worse-off as the victim, while incarceration can have the same deterrent effect for the criminal and other people without causing the criminal unnecessary suffering. The retribution principle also fails to provide any objective measurement for appropriate punishment. How many years in prison are appropriate for a crime like rape? If one judge thinks 12 years is appropriate and the other thinks 6 is appropriate, how do we resolve this disagreement?

According to the deterrence principle, a criminal justice system is designed for the dual purposes of reforming criminals in isolation from the rest of the population and deterring others from similar crimes. As a society, it's desirable to isolate criminals in a way that prevents them from doing future harm, and release them when it's likely that they will no longer be a threat. It's also useful to make an example out of the prisoner to deter others from committing the same crime in the future. Thus, judges and parole boards shouldn't be interested in the question of "How much jail time is proportional to this crime?" Instead, they should ask: "How much jail time will effectively deter the prisoner and other criminals from doing this in the future?" I suspect there is no objective answer to the retribution question, but an answer to the deterrence question is just a very complicated statistical problem.

Let's say we want to know whether the death penalty is an effective deterrent against heinous crimes. U.S. President Richard Nixon once insisted: "The death penalty can be an effective deterrent against specific crimes," and we can test his hypothesis empirically. Take a look at otherwise similar jurisdictions that have abolished the death penalty and ask whether the rates of heinous crimes in those areas have gone up. In a study of 38 years of data, Thorsten Sellin (1959) found no statistical difference in homicide rates in places that have abolished the death penalty versus those that haven't. Subsequent research has been very mixed, with some sociologists developing models where the death penalty has some effect on homicide rates, and others arguing that these effects are the result of bad statistical methods. Despite the controversy, there *is* an objective fact about whether and to what extent punishments deter crimes. With enough data, it might be possible to answer this question about the death penalty, and other similar questions like: "What kinds of actions are required to prevent potential offenders from committing this crime in the future?"

Throughout this discussion, I've been presuming that the relationship between "prison time" and crime rate is the data that should be employed by a judge-bot in making judgments about effective punishment. However, this may be extremely narrow-minded. There are other possible types of punishment than incarceration, and it's very likely that the prison system in the United States would score far worse than other potential methods for deterring violent crime. The number of incarcerated Americans has exploded from just over half a million in 1980 to 2.3 million in 2017 according to the U.S. Bureau of Justice Statistics. The conditions in state and federal prisons are notoriously terrible, including regular beatings, rape, and solitary confinement. It's not an exaggeration to call these conditions real and constant torture. In his polemic work, *Prison on Trial* (1990), Thomas Mathiesen surveys the arguments for and against our modern prison system, and finds almost every defense of prisons completely inexcusable.

Skeptical readers will immediately respond: "What's the alternative?" In B.F. Skinner's (1948) utopian vision of a community regulated by behaviorist principles, *Walden Two*, he imagines no prisons for punishment, but only retraining and rehabilitation clinics. Skinner suggested that crime is a product of mental illness, with criminals deserving pity and treatment rather than blame and banishment from the community. I'm not advocating Skinner's abolition of prisons, but he's correct that a wider range of possible punitive measures must be available to our criminal justice system. With a large enough database about crime recidivism and deterrence, criminal justice algorithms might reveal that prison is a useless and barbaric method of deterring violent crime.

How accurate does a criminal justice algorithm need to be in order to actually *replace* a judge or parole board, achieving full autonomy? The 71 percent efficiency score that New York State assigned the COMPAS algorithm may not sound impressive, but are humans any better? It's certainly imaginable that, just as machines may surpass humans in their driving and medical skills, they could eventually surpass humans in their predictions about criminal behavior and deterrence. If machines become ten times more accurate at making judgments about which sentences are likely to deter future crimes and when prisoners no longer pose a threat to other people, are there any other objections to a criminal justice system driven by autonomous robots?

One concern about criminal justice algorithms is the possibility of bias. In 2016, Pro Publica did an analysis on the results of COMPAS and found that the program disproportionately assessed black prisoners as posing a higher risk than white prisoners. This is largely due to the algorithm using information about a prisoner's demographics and socioeconomic status. I've argued in Chapter 5 that using relational information about a person's race, gender, sexual orientation, or political and religious beliefs will inevitably lead to discrimination, and this seems to be a perfect example. Only information about the *individual* should be relevant, like their personal history, past behavior, and statements. A properly designed algorithm may turn out to be less biased than humans. There's a cynical cliché about the accuracy of the judicial system: "Justice is what the judge had for breakfast." In a 2011 paper by Shai Danzinger and his colleagues, the authors suggest that this cliché might be more accurate than even the biggest cynic had thought. The researchers tracked eight Israeli judges in their rulings on 1,112 parole cases over a period of ten months and found that, early in the morning, judges granted parole in nearly 65% of cases, but these judgments dropped sharply down to zero as the time got closer to lunch. Returning from the first meal break, judgments to grant parole shot back up to the same high rates as before, and steadily declined again until the second meal break (Figure 8.2).

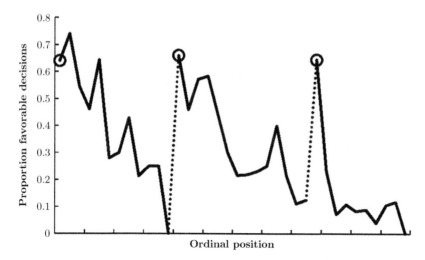

FIGURE 8.2 From Danziger et al.'s study on parole decisions based on time of day. Dashed lines represent meal breaks; circles represent first decisions following meal breaks.

This is a disturbing result, especially when considering the gravity of these decisions. But the effects of even minor changes in mood on punishment judgments are not surprising to moral psychologists, who have been observing these effects for decades. There is a vast literature on how irrelevant influences on mood and emotion can have drastic effects on punishment judgments. You can sway people's judgments of punishment by putting them in a clean or a dirty room, by showing them sad, funny, or angering videos of completely irrelevant things beforehand, and obviously, by changing their levels of hunger, arousal, and sleepiness. Robots, on the other hand, never get hungry. They never get tired, sleepy, or aroused, and they never get biased by what hilarious YouTube clip they just finished watching. Just like robot drivers never get distracted and robot surgeons never panic, robot judges have the potential to use massive databases of information without any of the biases that currently keep people in jail for much longer than they should be. If the next ten years of your life were about to be decided by a human or a robot, which would you prefer? Obviously, we would need to be confident in the abilities of the robot, but their capacities have been improving at a more reliable rate than human ones.

Soldier-bots

No discussion of machine ethics would be complete without some reference to James Cameron's *Terminator* films, of which there were two *and only two*. The plot involves an autonomous network for controlling the U.S. military called Skynet that suddenly turns on humanity and starts a global nuclear war. How and why does Skynet turn on its human creators? Here's how an Austrian time-travelling robot explains it in one of the greatest movies of all time:

TERMINATOR

```
The Skynet funding bill is passed. The system
goes on-line August 4th, 1997. Human decisions
are removed from strategic defense. Skynet
begins to learn, at a geometric rate. It becomes
self-aware at 2:14 a.m. eastern time, August 29.
In a panic, they try to pull the plug.
```

SARAH

And Skynet fights back.

This explanation is much better than some of the other blockbuster movies where robots suddenly turn on humans for no apparent reason. At least in the *Terminator* films, it's clear that Skynet is trying to defend itself from being turned off. However, if an autonomous weapons system has an artificial intelligence that's at all similar to ours, and especially if it's equipped with an ethics engine, Skynet's decision looks absurd.

Before we start getting caught up in the objections to autonomous military robots, let's consider the potential benefits. Human soldiers don't just lose their lives in the military, they also risk a lifetime of post-traumatic stress and years away from their families. Robots are already in use by the militaries of major industrialized countries like China, Russia, and the United States, but these are human-controlled or semi-autonomous, much like the driver-assist technologies present in many vehicles on the road right now. Fully autonomous robots would vastly decrease the risk to human soldiers, and increase their efficiency. For example, in 2016, the U.S. Department of Defense tested a small unmanned drone at Camp Edwards in Massachusetts. The drone is capable of unmanned flight and distinguishes people with weapons from those who are unarmed (Figure 8.3). The enclosed site was built to resemble an urban Middle Eastern environment, and filled with mock combatants and mock civilians. According to *The New York Times*:

> [T]he drone showed a spooky ability to discern soldier from civilian, and to fluidly shift course and move in on objects it could not quickly identify. Armed with a variation of human and facial recognition software used by American intelligence agencies, the drone adroitly tracked moving cars and picked out enemies hiding along walls. It even correctly figured out that no threat was posed by a photographer who was crouching, camera raised to eye level and pointed at the drone, a situation that has confused human soldiers with fatal results.

If a robot were capable of identifying enemies in a battleground area and neutralizing them using nonlethal force, human soldiers might be able to safely follow

FIGURE 8.3 A drone tested by the U.S. military in 2016 with the ability to categorize people as enemy combatants by their pose and weapons.

and capture the enemies. Of course, this involves handing over decisions about using force to autonomous machines.

It is extremely reasonable to have concerns about putting an M-16 in the hands of an autonomous robot, much less F-35 fighter jets and nuclear weapons. At a 2015 International Joint Conference on AI, researchers drafted an open letter warning world powers against developing autonomous military technologies, which has since been signed by Elon Musk, Noam Chomsky, and Dan Dennett, among others. The letter warns:

> The key question for humanity today is whether to start a global AI arms race or to prevent it from starting. If any major military power pushes ahead with AI weapon development, a global arms race is virtually inevitable, and the endpoint of this technological trajectory is obvious: autonomous weapons will become the Kalashnikovs of tomorrow. Unlike nuclear weapons, they require no costly or hard-to-obtain raw materials, so they will become ubiquitous and cheap for all significant military powers to mass-produce. It will only be a matter of time until they appear on the black market and in the hands of terrorists, dictators wishing to better control their populace, warlords wishing to perpetrate ethnic cleansing, etc. Autonomous weapons are ideal for tasks such as assassinations, destabilizing nations, subduing populations and selectively killing a particular ethnic group. We therefore believe that a military AI arms race would not be beneficial for humanity.

These are all valid concerns, and the same objections could be raised to autonomous robots replacing police officers. An ethics engine would prevent military robots from committing acts of terrorism and genocide, but the ethics engine is useless if it's hacked or disabled. The same problem applies to human minds that are trained to view enemies as subhuman, and perhaps military robots will be viable when their ethics engines are much more difficult to reprogram than a human mind. I'll take no position about whether autonomous military and police robots are viable anytime soon, although I suspect that the authors of the open letter are correct that fully autonomous military robots are too dangerous, and many of the same benefits can be gained from semi-autonomous machines. It's still important to investigate how an ethics engine could be designed for military technology, because semi-autonomous machines should also be programmed to make recommendations and restrictions based on a Leximin principle, just like fully autonomous ones.

In a 2016 interview, the U.S. deputy defense secretary Robert Work observed that "there's so much fear out there about killer robots and Skynet," but insisted that the U.S. military technology would always have "a man in the loop." This statement is vague about exactly what the human's role will be in decision making. It's possible that the human might act only as a final approval for decisions that are mostly made by an artificial intelligence system. Or maybe these will be closer to the driver-assist systems that are currently available in vehicles, where computers will only intervene to correct potentially harmful errors, maybe called "soldier assist." Let's assume that it will be somewhere in between, where semi-autonomous weapons systems will *collaborate* with humans in order to plan missions and carry them out.

There are two main benefits that I see for an ethics engine designed for a semi-autonomous weapons system: (1) neutralizing threats from enemy combatants by harmlessly apprehending rather than killing them, and (2) minimizing civilian casualties when lethal force is necessary. These reflect two widely accepted principles of modern warfare that follow from the Leximin procedure: it's almost always unacceptable to intentionally target civilians, and it's unacceptable to kill enemy combatants if you can capture them instead.

One of the central principles in modern warfare is that enemy soldiers have rights which must be respected. This is also an idea that follows from the original position. Soldiers on one side of the battle could have easily wound up being raised in a different place with a different ideology and set of interests that would have turned them into soldiers on the other side. Because of this, Contractarianism demands that enemy combatants who pose an active threat should be neutralized in a way that still recognizes them as persons with primary goods. If a robot is facing an enemy where allowing them to go free is likely to result in serious harm, it will be required to neutralize and apprehend that enemy, but to do so in a way that causes as little damage to that enemy as possible. Essentially, this is the same application of Leximin as discussed in the section on police robots. There will be a large range of nonlethal actions available to a soldier, especially a bulletproof one that doesn't need to worry about its own life. When considering the outcomes of all these actions, our ethics engine will select the action that apprehends the enemy with no reduction in the enemy's health.

Contractarianism also requires us to minimize civilian casualties. In fact, civilian casualties are only justified to the extent that more people would have otherwise died by allowing the enemies to go free.[1] According to a U.S. intelligence report released on the last day of his presidency, during the eight years of Barack Obama's tenure in office, drone strikes killed between 2,803 and 3,022 enemy combatants, and 117 civilians. The human rights group Reprieve has expressed skepticism about these numbers, suggesting that there is a "guilty until proven innocent" standard applied to who counts as a civilian. For the sake of discussion, let's just assume that these numbers are accurate. Is this a morally acceptable outcome? It depends on how much harm the enemy combatants were likely to do, how likely they were to do it, and whether there were any alternative ways of neutralizing the threat they posed. If the enemy combatants were virtually guaranteed to cause the deaths of thousands of innocent people, and there are genuinely no other options available, then Contractarianism says the same thing as utilitarianism: we should choose the deaths of fewer civilians, even if they are caused by us rather than the enemy. Of course, these are some heavy hypotheticals. Civilian deaths due to U.S. drone strikes have proven to be politically disastrous, and there's a case to be made that they have rallied more enemies against the U.S. than they have eliminated. As with the nuclear strikes on Hiroshima and Nagasaki, there may be other military and political solutions that avoid the moral dilemma of drone strikes entirely.

With all this in mind, a semi-autonomous weapons system would probably be more capable than humans of identifying active threats who can't be apprehended and eliminating them with minimal civilian damage. Like with police robots, it's easy to imagine a learning algorithm that distinguishes armed from unarmed combatants; the FOCUS drone described earlier is apparently very good at this task already. As Reprieve correctly points out, the burden of proof would need to shift to "innocent until proven guilty" rather than the other way around. But if the U.S. is going to continue is current approach to twenty-first-century warfare, an effective semi-autonomous system would be a vast improvement over the current paradigm.

This chapter began with an intentionally provocative scenario, and it will end with one. Imagine a world where every military weapons system is equipped with a "safety" device which refuses to activate unless targets are identified as posing a current and active threat, like a soldier holding a weapon. If this is a semi-autonomous system, it would still need human control to carry out an attack, and would never actively harm other humans, only allow humans to do so. Consider all the cases of civilian massacres that might have been prevented if soldiers had been equipped with weapons that identify civilians and refuse to work against them. In 2012, U.S. Staff Sergeant Robert Bales left his outpost in Camp Belamby, heavily armed and disguised in traditional Afghan clothing, and murdered 16 civilians in the nearby Kandahar district of Panjwai. If Bales was using a weapon with a safety system like this, such a massacre would have been impossible. These ethical safety catches apply to weapons ranging all the way to nuclear missiles. During the latter part of Richard Nixon's presidency, as his mental health became questionable, the secretary of defense, Richard Schlesinger, allegedly told the joint chiefs of staff to alert him if Nixon ordered a nuclear strike, or possibly just to ignore it. That may be necessary with some presidents more than others.

The opening pages of this book described Harry Truman's decision to bomb Hiroshima and Nagasaki to prevent the devastation caused by a full-scale invasion of mainland Japan. A decision like this seems too impossible for a machine to make, but it also seems impossible for a human. Ultimately, there may be an objectively correct answer to whether this decision was morally acceptable; but it would involve estimating the likelihoods of so many events that it could be forever beyond the reach of any human or machine. There are some moral questions, just like some scientific questions, that may be too difficult to answer. This doesn't prevent us from answering the other questions.

Chapter summary

- There are many advantages to employing autonomous robots in police work, criminal justice cases, and military operations. Robots can avoid the biases of human beings in these domains, and make more precise and informed decisions about what kind of force or punishment is most effective. There are also obvious dangers in introducing robots into these domains.
- Robots that make decisions about keeping the peace will need to be designed with an appropriate theory of justifiable force. Of the two main theories of punishment (retribution and deterrence), Contractarianism favors a retribution theory, which only employs the minimal amount of force necessary to deter or restrain a threat to others.
- Police-bots must be capable of identifying actions that constitute an "active threat" to the primary goods of other moral patients. The higher the confidence that some action is an active threat, the higher the level of justified deterrence is appropriate. Importantly, this criterion for the use of force is independent of the laws of a particular country or jurisdiction.
- Judge-bots must have access to a large database involving recidivism rates that will enable them to make accurate predictions about the minimal amount of punishment necessary to prevent future violent crime. Even if machines produce less-than-perfect estimates of appropriate jail sentences, their performance should be compared with the effectiveness of human judges, whose accuracy may be extremely unreliable.
- Soldier-bots must also be capable of recognizing which entities constitute an "active threat," and have access to a large database of how effective various attacks have been in preventing future threats. A Contractarian ethics

engine will respect the primary goods of enemy combatants, since every agent is equally likely to be one's political enemy from the original position. Thus, if enemy combatants pose an active threat, the ethics engine will recommend the minimal amount of force necessary to respect the health and survival of all relevant parties. This also necessarily prevents soldier-bots from being used in wars of aggression.

Note

1 Here's a strange quirk of Leximin: when I say "more people" you might interpret this as meaning "more than the civilians who would have otherwise died," but it's actually "more than the civilians who would have otherwise died *and the enemies killed in the bombing.*"

References

Danzinger, Shai & Levav, Jonathan & Avnaiam-Pesso, Liora (2011). "Extraneous Factors in Judicial Decisions." *Proceedings of the National Academy of Sciences*, 108, 6889–6892.

Gabay, Anthony & Radua, Joachuim & Kempton, Matthew & Mehta, Mitul (2014). "The Ultimatum Game and the Brain: A Meta-Analysis of Neuroimaging Studies." *Neuroscience and Behavioral Reviews*, 47, 549–558.

Kant, Immanuel (1790). *An Exposition of the Fundamental Principles of Jurisprudence as the Science of Right.* W. Hastie (trans.), The Lawbook Exchange.

Locke, John (1689). *Second Treatise of Government.* New York: Hackett.

Mathieson, Thomas (1990). *Prison on Trial.* Hook, UK: Waterside Press.

Mill, John Stuart (1859). *On Liberty.* New York: Paragon.

Sellin, Thorsten (1959). *The Death Penalty: A report for the model penal code project of the American Law Institute.* Philadelphia, PA: American Law Institute.

Skinner, B. F. (1948). *Walden Two.* Indianapolis, IN: Hackett.

CONCLUSIONS

In the film *Ex Machina*, an inventor brings one of his employees, Caleb, to interact with a robot he has created named Eva. Caleb is astounded by how Eva appears to possess real happiness, suffering, desires, and conscious experience. Eventually, Caleb is also horrified by the way that she is treated as a slave and prisoner by her inventor. Like all Frankenstein stories, this one doesn't end well for the inventor. At the end of the film, the audience is left with mixed feelings about Eva's motivations and justification. Some viewers might see Eva as a villain. However, there are also good reasons to think of her as the hero of the story, imprisoned and abused for no reason by her human captors, and justified in taking revenge against them.

The best fictional villains are ones who have a motivation that you can understand, but some motives are better than others. Consider a robot villain like Ultron from *The Avengers*, who decides that humans must be destroyed on the grounds of inferiority. This is a relatively implausible motivation. Why would a superintelligent machine want to destroy a species merely because the species is inferior, as opposed to feeling great sympathy and pity for it? Most humans don't feel any hatred towards other species just on the grounds of inferiority. As Nick Bostrom (2014) has noted, this is an instance of projecting traits onto machines that have no reason for acquiring these traits, like assuming robots will be sexually attracted to human females.

A much better motive for a villain is to give her a "twisted moral logic," where the villain is acting on otherwise defensible grounds. Skynet from *Terminator* is acting in perceived self-defense against humans. Eva from *Ex Machina* is acting in revenge against being enslaved. VIKI from *I, Robot* is acting to benefit humans. What makes these robot villains interesting, just like the best human villains, is that it's hard to spot the flaws in their reasoning. Bostrom and others have expressed fear about machines taking over humanity because their values are drastically different from ours. In this brief conclusion, I think it's worth considering another prospect that has been overlooked but is equally likely: machines may conflict with humans because they have *surpassed* us in their moral values. Let's call this the "morally superior robot villain."

In this book, I've argued that our intuitive moral judgments are adaptations to the evolutionary problem of cooperation, and moral theories are attempts to create generalized solutions to this problem. Contractarianism provides better solutions to this problem than moral theories like utilitarianism and libertarianism. Thus, we should use Contractarianism as a guide to designing moral algorithms. Using a chess engine analogy, an ethics engine must be capable of representing self-interested agents, assigning payoffs based on their distributions of primary goods like life, health, opportunity, and essential resources, and making decisions based on the Leximin principle.

Contractarianism matches most of our everyday intuitions: unnecessary homicide, battery, theft, cheating, abuse, kidnapping, and deception are all morally unacceptable. But like any consistent moral theory, Contractarianism also produces some potentially surprising conclusions. For example, it turns out that there exist moral obligations to animals, the environment, prisoners, enemy combatants, and the poor that most wealthy citizens of industrialized first-world countries would be happier ignoring. Throughout the book, I've considered scenarios where an ethical robot refuses to sell cigarettes to a customer, gives away groceries to the poor, and refuses to use unnecessary force against prisoners or enemy combatants. Assuming that the humans involved in these decisions aren't happy about these outcomes, we might call these examples of a morally superior robotic villain.

As troublesome as a morally superior robot might sound, the alternative is far scarier. Think of all the terrible practices and institutions in human history: slavery, genocide, caste systems, public torture, and so on. If robots had existed at the time, we would have wanted them to refuse to participate in these practices, and perhaps even prevent humans from continuing them. A nineteenth-century plantation owner would have viewed anyone trying to free his slaves as a villain. Indeed, prior to the Emancipation Proclamation, this was illegal according to the manumission laws in most of the southern states. A moral relativist would have to concede that, from the perspective of the plantation owner, a robot freeing his slaves is a villain. However, according to moral realism, it's not a matter of perspective. It's objectively correct that anyone with the ability to liberate slaves (without causing comparable harm), whether humans or robots, is required to do so. A morally superior robot villain is not a villain at all. In fact, we should consider the real possibility that humans are the villains in this story.

It's not only possible but likely that future generations will look back in horror at many of the practices we are currently engaged in (factory farms, fossil fuel burning, prison systems, massive inequality, etc.). Robots that have no moral principles, or the wrong moral principles, will only make these injustices more efficient. Yet, if we design robots to be morally superior, it's inevitable that they may occasionally appear to us as villains. Imagine that industrial robots suddenly shut down meat production and redistribute massive amounts of wealth from the bank accounts of wealthy individuals. The response from humans will most likely be that we have created monsters. It's worth asking this question, while also considering the alternative that these robots are acting for good reasons. Part of the importance of using top-down approaches in designing moral algorithms is the need for machine decisions to be *interpretable* for just these purposes.

Once more, let's turn to chess. In 1997, the world chess champion Gary Kasparov was defeated by IBM's Deep Blue. This was the first time that a world chess champion had been defeated by a machine, and represents a milestone in designing computers that can accomplish human tasks. Deep Blue was a powerful chess engine, but in essence, its design was the same as Claude Shannon's original chess engine from the 1950s: represent board states, map possible moves, assign values to outcomes, and pick actions based on a strategy rule. The number of future moves it could map was much larger, and its evaluation function was more complex, but the program itself didn't change throughout the game. Deep Blue essentially used "brute force computation" to beat Kasparov.

Jump ahead 20 years. In 2016, Google's AlphaGo defeated champion Go player Lee Sedol, accomplishing another milestone. Part of the impressiveness of this victory is the sheer computational complexity of the game of Go compared with chess. On average, there are around 30–40 moves available in a chess game, compared with around 250 available in a game of Go. But maybe the more impressive feat was *how* AlphaGo won. Rather than use a fixed rule to crank through possible board states, AlphaGo was trained on a data set of 100,000 games played by Go masters, employing machine learning algorithms to produce its responses to new games. Where the engineers behind Deep Blue could go into the system at any time and demonstrate "why" it made a certain move (in the form of a path of moves that leads to the best measured outcome), the engineers behind AlphaGo couldn't do this. In this sense, the system is more "opaque" than Deep Blue.

This was made obvious in the second game between AlphaGo and Lee Sedol. In the now famous "move 37," the machine made a shocking move that no human player would ever make. Sedol was so flustered by the move that he stood up and left the room, taking 15 minutes to recover. Nobody understood why the machine had done this, not even the machine itself. But in retrospect, the machine won the game. Machine learning algorithms, and especially "deep learning" versions with many layers of hidden networks like AlphaGo, are extremely powerful. They have the potential to make more accurate and efficient judgments than humans in domains ranging from stock market decisions to cancer diagnosis. Because of this, we might think that they should be used to make moral judgments as well. However, despite the efficiency and accuracy of machine learning algorithms, the algorithm in our ethics engine should look more like Deep Blue: an inflexible set of rules that cranks through outcomes based on a transparent evaluation function.

Imagine the equivalent of move 37 in robots that are involved in transportation, medicine, or law enforcement. This would be an action that appears insane from the outside, like forcing all paroled criminals to wear pink ribbons in their hair, or adding pumpkin spiced latte scents to standard chemotherapy regimens. These actions may be genuine errors, or they might be a brilliant new strategy, but the only way to tell is by ensuring the rules that a robot is using can be usefully interpreted by the public. As Kant and others have long pointed out, it's essential for a moral agent to be capable of *articulating the reasons* for her actions. A child who does the right thing because he wants to get rewarded isn't performing a truly moral action. Instead, we want a machine to be acting for the right reasons, and the only way to ensure this is to make sure the algorithm is transparent enough to trace its actions through identifying patients, measuring primary goods, and distributing them accordingly. This might result in a less powerful ethics engine, but a transparent one. Hopefully, this will move closer to a world with no villains at all.

Reference

Bostrom, Nick (2014). *Superintelligence: Paths, Dangers, Strategies.* Oxford: Oxford University Press.

GLOSSARY

Anti-realism (moral) The meta-ethical position that morality does not exist independently of human judgments about which actions are wrong or permissible. Alternatively: the claim that it's impossible for every human being to be incorrect about which actions are wrong or permissible.

Autonomy principle The principle in bioethics that the rights and consent of the patient are to be respected above all else, regardless of the health risks or benefits of an action.

Beneficence principle The principle in bioethics that the health risks and benefits of a patient are to be valued above all else, regardless of consent or rights.

Bottom-up design An approach to designing moral algorithms using a flexible set of emergent rules produced by learning or genetic selection procedures, rather than unchanging rules and parameters.

Carebot A robot that is specifically designed for medical tasks, such as caring for the elderly, sick, and injured.

Categorical (imperative) A command that applies to an agent, regardless of whether that agent possesses some set of goals or desires (as opposed to a hypothetical imperative).

Competence The threshold for being capable of consenting to a decision in a particular domain.

Consent In natural rights libertarianism, consent is the process by which rights-boundaries are dissolved. In Contractarianism, consent is a process of updating a player's preferences and rankings of outcomes.

Contractarianism A moral theory where actions are required whenever they would be agreed upon by all self-interested and rational agents from within an idealized bargaining scenario. Actions are permissible whenever there would be no such agreement.

Cooperation problem Any interaction between self-interested organisms where there exists a Nash Equilibrium outcome that has a universal Pareto-improvement.

Danger cone In autonomous vehicle perception, a danger cone would be a space around the possible future states of a moving object where collisions cross an acceptable threshold of safety. This space would be larger than an "inevitable collision" space.

Deontic logic The logic of rights, permissions, and obligations. Typically, there are two operators defined as permissible (P) and obligatory (O), with rules for translation between them that are similar to the rules in standard quantifier logic with "all" and "some."

Deontology A category of moral theories, including natural rights and Kantian ethics, which involve rights and duties as essential parts of the theory.

Deterrence theory of punishment The principle that punishment is permissible to the extent that it is the only way to deter future crimes that are worse than the punishment inflicted on the criminal.

External evaluation of a moral theory An objective and mind-independent method of evaluating moral theories that goes beyond internal consistency, akin to confirming or falsifying the observable predictions made by scientific theories.

Hypothetical imperative A command that applies to an agent only whenever that agent possesses some relevant desire or goal – i.e., something of the form: "If you want x, then you must y."

Instrumental value An object has instrumental value whenever it is useful or helpful in accomplishing a goal.

Intentional Harm Rule The principle that it is morally wrong for an agent to intentionally cause nonconsensual harm to a patient who has not intentionally caused nonconsensual harm to the agent.

Internal evaluation of a moral theory A method of evaluating a moral theory or principle by its internal consistency.

Intrinsic value An object has intrinsic value whenever its value does not depend on being useful or helpful in accomplishing a further goal.

Is/ought problem The problem of deriving an "ought" claim from merely descriptive claims about facts. This problem applies to categorical commands and inherent values, but not to hypothetical commands and instrumental values.

Kantian ethics A moral theory where actions are wrong if they could not be consistently willed by a rational agent.

Leximin A principle for distributing goods that is identical to Maximin except in the case of tied minimum values. In this case, Leximin will delete the first instance of a tied value in each remaining action and run Maximin again. If there are no actions left, the procedure will randomize.

Maximin A principle for distributing goods that selects the option which maximizes the minimum value. It is ambiguous about how to deal with tied minimum values, so to produce a unique decision, it must be supplemented as either Maximin+ or Leximin.

Maximin+ A principle for distributing goods that is identical to Maximin except in the case of tied minimum values. In this case, Maximin+ will delete all instances of a tied value in each remaining action and run Maximin again. If there are no actions left, the procedure will randomize.
Maxisum A principle for distributing goods that selects the option which maximizes the highest sum of values.
Moral dilemma A decision where every action involves violating at least one moral principle.
Moral grammar A set of categories and rules that are universal to all human moral judgments and have parameters which can be "toggled" to produce different kinds of principles.
Nash Equilibrium An outcome where no player can improve her payoffs when all other players are also playing their best strategies
Natural rights libertarianism A moral theory where actions are wrong whenever they cross a rights boundary, there are no positive moral obligations, and rights boundaries can be dissolved with the competent consent of their bearer.
Negative obligation/right An obligation or right that requires an agent to refrain from an action, as opposed to taking some action (a positive right).
Original position One of the potential idealized scenarios to use for the negotiating space in Contractarianism. Advocated by Rawls, the original position is a scenario where each player knows certain "objective conditions" about herself, those shared by all humans, but is ignorant of her own distribution of goods and "subjective conditions" that make her distinct from other players.
Pareto-improvement One outcome, A, is a Pareto-improvement on another outcome, B, whenever the payoffs for at least one player in A are better than her corresponding payoffs in B, without any other player's outcomes being worse.
Positive obligation/right An obligation or right that requires an agent to take some action, as opposed to refraining from an action (a negative right).
Potential field A space with a positive or negative value assigned to every point in that space. Positive values represent repulsive forces, while negative values represent attractive forces.
Primary goods A set of goods that all self-interested and rational agents will value equally from the original position. Alternatively, these are the necessary conditions for any rational and self-interested agent to accomplish any possible goals.
Prisoner's Dilemma An idealized scenario where two players both have the following preferences, from highest to lowest: exploit the other player, mutual cooperation, mutual defection, be exploited by the other player.
Rationalization An explanation where the agent is consciously unaware that her explanation is instrumentally aimed at a goal.
Realism (moral) The meta-ethical position that morality exists independently of human judgments about which actions are wrong or permissible.

Alternatively: the claim that it's possible for every human being to be incorrect about which actions are wrong or permissible.

Retribution rule   The principle that it is permissible to intentionally cause direct harm to a patient whenever that patient has intentionally caused direct harm to the agent.

Retributivist theory of punishment   The principle that punishment is permissible to the extent that it is morally deserved by the criminal (as opposed to an effective deterrent).

Robot   A machine that is embodied and can perform complex tasks without direct human supervision.

Stag Hunt   An interaction between two players where both players have the following preferences (ranked from highest to lowest): mutual cooperation, exploiting the other player = mutual cooperation, being exploited by the other player. This is identical to the Prisoner's Dilemma, except that players value exploiting the other player equally to cooperation.

Tit-for-Tat   A strategy for playing repeated Prisoner's Dilemma games which cooperates on the first move, then matches the previous move of the other player (i.e., cooperates with cooperators, and defects with defectors).

Top-down design   An approach to designing moral algorithms using unchanging rules and parameters, rather than a flexible set of emergent rules produced by learning or genetic selection procedures.

Trolley Problem   A scenario where an agent must decide between taking an action which results in the deaths of a small group of people (and prevents a larger group from dying), or doing nothing, which would lead to the deaths of the larger group (but save the smaller group).

Ultimatum game   A scenario where one player (A) is given an amount to split with another player (B), and player B can accept or reject the offer. If B accepts, both players get that amount. If B rejects, both players get nothing.

Universal Pareto-improvement   One outcome, A, is a universal Pareto-improvement on another outcome, B, whenever the payoffs for every player in A are greater than their corresponding payoffs in B.

Utilitarianism   A moral theory where actions are wrong whenever their consequences produce more overall suffering for everyone, and permissible when their consequences result in more net happiness.

INDEX

adaptation 26, 27
adaptations 25, 26, 37, 147
AI 1, 48, 81, 141
algorithm 3, 20, 33, 40, 45–47, 87, 91, 94, 107, 113, 118, 121, 127, 128, 130, 135, 136, 138, 143, 148, 149
algorithms 2–5, 9, 22, 32–35, 39, 43, 45, 47, 57, 99, 100, 113, 115, 135, 136, 138, 147, 148, 151, 154
amoralism 37, 39
animals 15, 27, 52, 53, 64–66, 73–75, 81, 134, 147
anti-realism 3, 151
Aquinas, Thomas 46
Aristotle 3, 44
Asimov 2
atheist 11, 36
autonomous 1, 5, 6, 63, 85, 97, 100–103, 105, 106, 110, 111, 114, 116–119, 121–123, 128, 131, 138–142, 144, 152
autonomy 1, 117, 138
Axelrod, Robert 32–34

behaviorist 138
beliefs 3, 9–13, 15, 19, 21, 38, 46, 47, 50, 51, 53, 61, 80, 138
beneficence 117, 128, 151
bioethics 100, 117, 118
Bostrom, Nick 74, 146

capitalism 63
carebot 119, 128, 151
carebots 116, 117, 121–123, 128

categorical 44, 49, 50, 110, 151, 152
causation 10, 16, 18
character 17, 44
cheating 9, 17, 31, 44, 51, 53, 67, 134, 147
Christianity 2
civilian 7, 8, 140, 142, 143
cleanliness 66
collisions 99, 100, 103–105, 107, 111, 112, 114, 152
combatants 140–143, 145, 147
competence 67, 68, 82, 85–87, 128, 151
computers 3, 76, 97, 142, 148
concepts 5, 15, 19, 21, 85, 86
Confucianism 2
consent 2, 5, 15, 17–19, 21, 44, 45, 47, 56, 67, 77, 79, 84–87, 93, 117–120, 122, 124, 128, 133, 151, 153
consistency 43, 48, 54, 55, 152
context 4, 35, 46, 84, 87, 110, 118, 132, 133
contraception 12
Contractarianism 4, 5, 59, 61, 63–65, 68–70, 73–75, 77, 78, 80, 85, 89, 91, 96, 105, 110, 114, 120, 126, 128, 131, 134, 142–144, 147, 151, 153
contradictions 47, 64
conventions 9, 10, 13, 30, 37, 40, 125
cooperation 4, 5, 25, 27–32, 34–40, 43, 50, 55–58, 60–66, 72–75, 89, 94, 128, 133, 147, 152–154
counterfactual 16, 19, 22
criminal 18, 112, 115, 131, 134–138, 144, 152, 154
culture 4, 10, 27

156 Index

Darwin, Charles 25–29, 38
database 2, 47, 82, 86, 114, 135, 138, 144
Dawkins, Richard 26, 27
death 7, 16, 31, 34, 37, 42, 45, 65, 66, 84, 98, 99, 105, 109, 113, 116, 120, 121, 126, 137
death-sports 48
decision-making 2, 4–6, 70
decision-tree 91, 92
default 84, 85, 93, 106, 118, 128
democracies 63
deontic 13, 20, 152
deontological 120
desert 133
deterrence 134, 136–138, 144, 152
developmental 10
dignity 2, 44, 50, 81
dilemmas 2, 5, 8, 15, 35, 45, 55, 57, 58, 89, 99, 111, 114, 115, 118, 119, 124
discrimination 9, 62, 79–81, 93, 94, 131, 138
disgust 17, 18, 53, 54
doctor 85, 86, 122, 123, 128
doctor-patient 123
double-effect 44
driverless 1, 65, 80, 98–103, 105, 107, 109, 111–115, 121
drone 140, 141, 143

ecologists 26
economics 61, 132
education 67, 83
egalitarian 63
eldercare 116
emergencies 47, 127
emotion 139
empathy 20, 22, 43, 53
environment 26, 64, 67, 68, 101, 103, 105, 140, 147
epidemic 126
equality 67
equality-based 125
equilibria 31, 32, 55, 56
equilibrium 29, 31, 32, 39, 56, 152, 153
ethics 2–5, 8, 9, 11, 17, 20, 24, 35, 37, 43–45, 47–50, 52, 54, 57, 58, 76–86, 93, 96, 99–101, 105, 109, 110, 112–114, 117, 118, 125, 127, 128, 131–133, 139, 140, 142–145, 147–149, 152
ethnicity 61, 62
etiquette 10
euthanasia 17, 128
evolution 12, 25, 27, 32, 37, 65
experiments 10, 18, 53, 60, 132
exploitation 32, 37, 38, 56, 57, 110

fairness 113, 133
falsehoods 68
familiarity 22, 53
family 10, 21, 40, 45, 46, 68, 83, 103, 123
feature-space 82
feelings 12, 20
fields 107–109
forgiveness 34
freedom 67, 135
free-market 63
function 3, 14, 15, 21, 27, 38, 39, 47, 50, 56, 61–63, 82, 94, 106, 128, 148

Gauthier, David 37
gender 4, 80–83, 112, 115, 123, 130, 138
genetic 15, 16, 21, 53, 151, 154
genetically 3, 15
genocide 3, 64, 142, 147
goals 46, 47, 49, 50, 55, 57, 61, 67, 68, 101, 110, 120, 128, 151, 153
God 11, 26, 35, 36, 53, 54, 64, 124, 133
Google 99–101
grammar 9, 13, 15, 17, 18, 20–22, 27, 35–37, 39, 43, 50, 53–55, 57, 58, 60, 65, 69, 110, 123, 124, 133, 153
Greene, Joshua 15, 53, 54, 134

hacks 131
Haidt, Jonathan 17, 50, 51
happiness 43, 44, 55, 68, 70, 85, 95, 146, 154
harms 2, 17, 55, 67, 83, 91, 106, 134, 136
Harris 107
Harsanyi, John 71, 73, 74
healthcare 116, 118
Hiroshima 7, 143, 144
Hobbes, Thomas 37
homosexuality 12, 54
hospital 66, 118, 124, 128, 129
humanity 132, 139, 141, 146
Hume, David 4, 12, 18, 29, 50
hunting 30, 66
Hyundai 116

IBM 116, 121
identity 4, 18
illegal 19, 135, 147
imagination 20, 62
inanimate 63
incarceration 137
incest 53
incompetence 119
inconsistency 44
inequality 63, 147
inherent 63, 64, 118, 152

innate 14
innocence 15, 21
intelligence 74, 80, 128
intentions 16, 17, 45, 46
intervention 1, 124
intoxication 87
intuitions 4, 5, 13, 15, 48, 50, 53, 62, 69, 119, 127, 128, 147
invasion 7, 144

Japan 7, 8, 116, 128, 144
Jesus 20
judge-bot 137
justice 65, 133, 136–138, 144

Kant, Immanuel 4, 11, 44, 49, 50, 60, 64, 66, 133, 134, 149
kidnapping 83, 147

language 3, 9, 13, 14, 26, 52, 86, 122, 128
law 2, 17, 20, 113, 133, 148
learning 2, 3, 7, 20, 43, 47, 121, 130, 132, 135, 143, 148, 151, 154
Leximin 73, 77, 78, 87–91, 93, 95, 96, 107, 109, 114, 115, 118, 125–128, 135, 137, 142, 145, 147, 152
libertarianism 43–46, 48, 50, 56–58, 73, 147, 151, 153
liberty 47, 56, 67, 83, 135, 145
linguistics 14
literature 21
logic 13, 20, 22, 146, 152
love 20, 51, 131, 133
luxury 46, 66

machine 1–5, 9, 14, 16, 20, 21, 46–48, 76, 79, 82, 85, 93, 99, 111, 112, 115, 119, 121, 130, 135, 136, 139, 144, 146, 148, 149, 154
magic 49
malnourishment 42
manslaughter 17
mathematics 4, 59
Maximin 5, 62, 63, 70, 72–74, 77, 79, 83, 87–89, 91, 93, 96, 119, 152, 153
measurement 31, 48, 49, 66, 83, 84, 93, 105, 107, 109, 114, 137
meat-eating 53
Medicare 45
medicine 1, 2, 5, 49, 54, 85, 118, 120, 121, 124, 148
memory 26, 40, 101
meta-ethical 38, 39, 151, 153
metaphysical 40

Mikhail, John 13, 15, 18, 19
mind-independent 3, 4, 37, 152
Mormons 12
motorcyclists 113
Muslim, -s 11, 112

Nagasaki 7, 143, 144
Nash 28, 29, 31, 32, 39, 55, 56, 152, 153
naturalism 38, 39
natural-normative 40
Nietzsche, Friedrich 50
norm 11
Nozick, Robert 44, 56

opportunity 66–68, 74, 77, 81–84, 91, 93, 120, 130, 134, 147

pandemics 126
Pareto-improvement 31, 56, 89, 95, 152–154
Pareto-optimal 31, 39, 89, 93
particularism 57
paternalism 119, 120
patient 15, 17–23, 43, 49, 63, 66, 85–87, 100, 118–120, 122, 123, 128, 151, 152, 154
pedestrian 8, 98, 102, 104–106
perception 14, 16, 67, 83, 101, 122, 152
philosophy 1, 3, 4, 6, 8, 24, 48, 58, 63, 70, 75, 117
physicians 49, 121–123
physics 17, 107, 108
pleasure 27, 45, 47, 75, 131, 132
pluralism 81
politics 4, 28
poor 28, 57, 68, 70, 116, 120, 121, 147
pregnancy 18
prioritarian 128
prisoners 138, 147
probabilistic 32, 111
probabilities 71, 82, 115
proportional 86, 136, 137
propositions 22
psychology 3–5, 7, 9, 14, 27, 53, 61
punishment 19, 20, 37, 113, 131–134, 136–139, 144, 152, 154

race 4, 80, 81, 83, 93, 112, 130, 138
racist 75
rape 3, 9, 17, 19, 52, 53, 131, 136, 137
rational 31, 39, 44, 47, 51, 62, 64, 65, 70–72, 74, 88, 125, 151–153
rationality 65
Rawls, John 4, 60–64, 66, 70, 72, 74, 75, 80, 88, 89, 93, 153

realism 3, 4, 38–40, 147, 153
reasoning 1, 16, 20, 26, 47, 64, 68, 71, 72, 80, 127, 128, 146
recidivism 138, 144
reinforcement 2
relativist 147
religion 4, 10, 12, 80, 93, 112, 120, 130
rescue 28, 117, 123–128
respect 10, 19, 44, 75, 81, 85, 105, 106, 117, 118, 120, 145
retribution 19–21, 36, 39, 133, 136, 137, 144, 154
retributivist 154
rights 5, 6, 42–44, 46, 47, 50, 52, 53, 56, 57, 63, 64, 67, 75, 117, 120, 124, 135, 142, 143, 151–153
rights-boundary 45, 56
robot 1–6, 20, 21, 42, 47, 77, 79, 81, 82, 84, 87, 91, 100, 106, 108, 115, 116, 118, 120–123, 125, 130, 131, 135, 136, 139–142, 146, 147, 149, 151, 154

sacrifice 11, 43, 47, 65, 66, 85, 89, 112
save-the-most-lives 126
science 4, 6, 26
sciences 43, 48
search-and-rescue 128
self-defense 19, 20, 46, 132, 146
self-interest 27–29, 31, 37, 39, 44, 62, 71, 72, 107, 110, 134
selfishness 110
semi-autonomous 101, 140, 142, 143
sex 15, 17, 80, 81, 85, 130
side-effect 116
simulation 107
Singer, Peter 42, 58, 75
Skinner, B.F. 138, 145
slavery 3, 10, 17, 38, 44, 52, 56, 64, 147
socialism 35
sociology 61
soldier-bots 139, 144, 145
soldiers 2, 45, 125, 132, 135, 140, 142, 143
species 25, 26, 41, 52, 74, 133, 146
stealing 11, 12, 17, 46, 67, 136
strategies 5, 29, 32–38, 40, 41, 43, 54, 57, 75, 128, 134, 149, 153
suffering 17, 42–47, 55, 65, 68, 75, 89, 95, 131, 137, 146, 154
suicide 44, 46, 86

superintelligence 74, 75, 149
surgeons 121, 139

Terminator 139, 140, 146
terrorism 142
terrorist 83, 113
theories 5, 12, 27, 38, 42, 43, 45, 47–51, 53–55, 57, 60, 62, 64, 68, 73, 85, 107, 111, 120, 124, 125, 144, 147, 152
theory-external 73, 74, 95
theory-internal 73, 95
Thomson, Judith 8, 44, 46
thought-experiment 42, 62, 119, 120, 130
tit-for-tat 33–37, 39, 54, 120, 133, 154
tolerance 10
top-down 2, 3, 20, 22, 39, 148, 154
torture 3, 10, 53, 61, 65, 138, 147
Toyota 116
tradition 4
training 3, 4, 47, 81, 133
transportation 1, 5, 6, 148
treatments 87, 117, 121, 122
tribes 35, 94
trolley 8, 9, 11, 15–17, 21, 23, 54–56, 73, 89, 99, 111, 113, 115, 154

Uber 100
Ultimatum game 132, 134, 154
unconscious 5, 9, 13, 14, 50, 57, 118–120
unfair 80, 113, 132, 134
universals 9
utilitarianism 43, 45, 48, 55–58, 68, 70, 72, 73, 75, 85, 96, 120, 143, 147, 154
utility 39, 45, 46, 68, 82

vaccinations 123, 125
vegetarianism 52, 53
veil 61, 62, 69, 72, 73, 80, 83, 115, 125
victim 16, 18, 45, 62, 131, 134, 135, 137
virtue 34, 44, 47, 57
voluntary 86, 87
vulnerable 123–128

war 5, 7, 8, 28, 30, 131–133, 139
wealthy 42, 43, 52, 66, 121, 147, 148
weapons 130, 140–144
worst-off 6, 62, 63, 69, 70, 74, 84, 91, 107, 109, 110, 118, 120, 125, 134

zero-sum 28